Biblical Healing

It is God's will for you to be well

Wendy Bowen

Biblical Healing

Manifest International, LLC

ISBN: 978-0-9978009-8-2

Scripture references in this book are from the New International Version of the Bible unless otherwise noted. Emphasis added by author for teaching purposes.

All Biblical definitions in this book are from Strong's Hebrew and Greek Lexicon, Gesenius' Hebrew-Chaldee Lexicon, and Thayer's Greek Lexicon

Please note that the names and references to God are capitalized to acknowledge and worship His deity. In contrast, the names and other references to satan are not capitalized, even to the point of violating grammatical rules, so as to equally acknowledge his position of defeat.

Cover Design: Don Patton, Photo credits: Kjpargeter/Freepik, Elaine Debroqc

Proofreading by Susan Williams and Bekah Brinkley

DEDICATION

To Jesus, for healing me.

CONTENTS

Biblical Healing
INTRODUCTION

Our God heals. Jesus Christ took ALL of our sicknesses upon Himself at the cross and nullified ALL of the enemy's assertions to the contrary. Healing was included in the price Jesus paid to redeem us as God's people and this makes healing our born-again birthright as His children. The only thing left for us to do is to believe what Jesus has done for us and to receive it for ourselves as a free gift.

This may sound over simplified, but I assure you it is not. Too often, we in the Church have made healing teachings too complicated because our experience does not match what we read in the Word of God. When we do this, we reframe the Scriptures and take them out of context to create doctrines which justify ourselves, our experiences, and our unbelief. Frequently, prayer methods and techniques are constructed, which good as they may seem, have unintentionally created rules and religion, which inherently disqualify us from free grace because they have shifted our faith from our Healer to our method. At other times, when it seems God is not supernaturally intervening to heal us, we become frustrated or overly passive in the name of *God's sovereignty*, rather than truly seeking to know Him as our Healer and actively engaging our faith to receive what He died to give us, even if it means repenting of wrong beliefs. However, healing comes when we know God through the righteousness Christ has provided for us. This means that we must be willing to have our minds, hearts, and lives changed in whatever ways necessary to bring our experience into alignment with God's Word rather than the other way around.

Some people struggle more with believing God for healing but most struggle more with receiving healing from God. The two are inextricably intertwined. Therefore, I believe that the Lord has led me to write this book in two sections: Believing and Receiving. The Believing section starts with the story of our redemption as children of God, using the

Passover as the prophetic shadow and springboard for our study. This section is dedicated to proving from the Scriptures in various ways that our healing is most definitely a finished work that Jesus paid for in full, without exception. Then, the Receiving section's purpose is to assist you in aligning yourself with the truth so that you can obtain healing for yourself. This includes practical applications for believing Jesus in addition to demolishing some erroneous arguments the enemy uses to keep God's people stuck in unbelief and infirmity. The chapters in the Believing section are longer and weightier, while the chapters of the Receiving section are shorter and punchier. Both sections are equally important to your healing and I strongly encourage you to read the whole book because questions raised as you read one section may very well be addressed in the other. Plus, there is no use dismantling wrong ideas unless they are replaced with truth and there is little value in knowledge of the Scriptures unless we take steps to put our faith into practice in our lives.

On that note, I also believe that the Lord has asked me to share more of my own testimonies in this book than any other book I have written to date. To start, you should know that several years ago, after pursing the Lord fairly intensely in the area of healing, He gave me such penetrating revelation of His healing as a part of our redemption that He also asked me to renounce all medicine and remedies in order to align my actions with my faith. After confirming that this was Him speaking to me, I swallowed with a hard gulp in my throat and said, "Yes, Lord." Please note, I do not teach that everyone should take the same approach, and we will cover this in a later chapter. This said, once I submitted myself in obedience to the Lord's instruction, I woke up the next morning completely healed of chronic severe allergies. I knew that this healing was confirmation of God's grace for me as I pursued experiential knowledge of Him as my one and only Healer. Leading up to this point, and even since then, the Lord has miraculously healed me of a variety of things from minor to life-threatening. I will share some of these experiences with you, mostly to encourage you in the struggle to maintain simple faith rather than being side-tracked by methods and approaches which wind up being self-focused, hyped-up, and lead to striving rather than child-like dependence. My heart for you in this book is to spare you the agony and frustration of chasing the wrong things so that you can focus your attention entirely on the one true thing: God's grace through faith in Jesus.

One more thing before we get started. In the Book of Job, after Job lost everything he had, including the unexpected deaths of his children, he mourned but did not give way to anger at God or any unrighteousness in his heart. Then, the evil one said something insightful about humans and our health.

> *Job 2:4-5 - "Skin for skin!" Satan replied [to God]. "A man will give all he has for his own life. But now stretch out your hand and strike his flesh and bones, and he will surely curse you to your face."*

Even though the devil is a liar and the father of lies, he is an expert at crafting lies that are based in truth. Truthfully, issues with our health do call our faith to the forefront and expose what we really believe. When our lives or way of life are affected by health issues, it can cause us to give way to unbelief and to question God's goodness. Our self-righteousness and wrong beliefs can be exposed as they prove fruitless in our pursuit of healing. Our selfishness in pursuing our own agenda for our lives rather than God's purposes can be revealed as our plans become stunted. All of this can lead to painful disillusionment, spiritual fatigue, and even anger at God. But it does not have to. If we believe correctly about who God is and what He has done for us by giving His Son, we can see the devil for the liar he is and not be shaken by any fiery dart he throws at us, even the threat of death.

With all of this said, I am almost certain that I will offend you at some point in this book. My aim is not to offend but to challenge you to go deeper in your faith and to help you to stand firm in the goodness of the Good News. Because of this, I cannot back down on what the Scriptures reveal about healing no matter what victories or failures you may have experienced or someone you know that died even though they seemed to have strong faith or led a Bible study. I'm deeply sorry for your loss, but it does not change God's will or negate that Jesus' stripes healed us at the cross. The Word of God is a double-edged sword that reveals the areas of our hearts where we are not at rest in Him so that we may repent and be healed. So, rather than being offended, I encourage you to ask the Holy Spirit to reveal truth to you so that you grow deeper in knowing and believing that it is God's will for you to be well. I have also assembled a selection of healing Scriptures and supplied them as an appendix at the end of this book.

For me, revelation that healing was included as a part of our redemption became a catalyst that accelerated my understanding of the Gospel and all Jesus truly did for us. I hope that it does the same for you. May this book circumcise your heart with the sword of God's Word so that you believe and receive everything Jesus attained for you.

Believing

Chapter One

A Redeemed People

Thousands of years ago, the one and only God, who is the Creator of heaven and earth, redeemed a people for Himself. His design was for them to be special to Him and unique among all the nations as the only people who worshiped Him and had a relationship with Him. His purpose was for them to be blessed above all other peoples with health, abundance, and supernatural strategies of war so that His goodness could be revealed through them to the rest of the world.

In one event, the Passover is the most poignant example of the whole story God is telling through the Scriptures from the Book of Genesis to the Book of Revelation. The events we read about in the Old Testament Scriptures are a prophetic shadow that reveals God's greater work of redemption and points us to His Son, Jesus Christ. (see Colossians 2:17) In other words, what we see in the Old Testament in the natural is what we have spiritually in the New Covenant. For example, in the Old Testament we see literal battles and wars in earthly territories whereas in the New Covenant our fight is not against flesh and blood but against spiritual forces of evil in heavenly places. (see Ephesians 6:12) In light of this, the Old Testament Passover reveals so much about what God has done for us as His children that whole books could be written about the many elements, types, and shadows presented in the original Exodus story and how they were fulfilled through Christ, our eternal Passover Lamb.

> *1 Corinthians 5:7b - For Christ, **our Passover lamb**, has been sacrificed.*
>
> *1 Peter 1:18-19 - For you know that it was not with perishable things such as silver or gold that you were redeemed from the empty way of life handed down to you from your ancestors, but with the precious blood of Christ, **a lamb without blemish or defect**.*

*John 1:29 - The next day John saw Jesus coming toward him and said, "Look, **the Lamb of God**, who takes away the sin of the world!*

Therefore, in this chapter, we will walk through the Passover story and the ways that it reveals God's work in setting us apart as His eternal people who are redeemed from sin, sickness, and death. First, we will review the original Passover, which is the smaller story of how God redeemed His people, Israel. Then we will walk through the eternal Passover, which is the larger story God is telling through the whole of Scripture about how He redeemed us to be His beloved children. Finally, we will highlight a few significant facets of God's redeeming work and the prophetic parallels between the two stories.

How is all of this significant for our healing in Christ? Well, when God redeemed the people of Israel and miraculously walked them through the Red Sea, not one of them was weak, sick, infirm, or feeble in any way. (see Psalm 105:37) Therefore, if this was the case in what was merely a prophetic shadow of God's greater work, then I submit to you that because of what Jesus did for us through His life, death, and resurrection, health and healing are our born-again birthright as children of God.

The First Passover (the Shadow)

Several hundred years before the first Passover, God selected a man named Abram/Abraham to be the head of a nation of people who were special to Him.

*Genesis 12:1-3 - The LORD had said to Abram, "Go from your country, your people and your father's household to the land I will show you. **I will make you into a great nation**, and I will bless you; I will make your name great, and you will be a blessing. I will bless those who bless you, and whoever curses you I will curse; and all peoples on earth will be blessed through you."*

At this point in time, nobody on earth had a relationship with the one true God and even Abraham lived in Ur, a city of Chaldeans who were known as astronomers and magicians who worshipped the sun, moon, and stars. But God called upon Abraham to leave the splendor of Ur in order to go to a land that God would show him and ultimately give to him. God promised Abraham a land, a people, and a blessing. At first, when Abraham set out to follow God's instructions, God's promises all seemed terribly unlikely because Abraham lived in tents as a nomad, had a barren wife, and probably appeared from the world's perspective to be a not-so-blessed wanderer. Nevertheless, Abraham believed God.

Many years later, Abraham still lived in tents in a land owned by someone else and had no children. At this point, God entered into a covenant with Abraham. A covenant is a binding agreement sealed with blood sacrifices, which was God's way of unconditionally guaranteeing that His promises would come to pass. God also revealed at this time that Abraham's descendants would be sold into slavery for a period of time but promised that He would redeem Abraham's people from slavery and give them the Promised Land. (see Genesis 15)

> *Genesis 15:13-16 - Then the LORD said to him, "Know for certain that for four hundred years* ***your descendants will be strangers in a country not their own and that they will be enslaved and mistreated there. But I will punish the nation they serve as slaves****, and afterward they will come out with great possessions. You, however, will go to your ancestors in peace and be buried at a good old age. In the fourth generation* ***your descendants will come back here****, for the sin of the Amorites has not yet reached its full measure."*

Quite a few more years later, Abraham still believed God even though he had no land and no heir from his wife who was still barren and had aged beyond her years of child bearing. This time, God assured Abraham that he would have a son through his wife and this son would be his heir. God also gave Abraham the terms for inclusion in His covenant. In order for anyone to be included in God's promises and blessings to Abraham, they had to be circumcised by cutting off the flesh of their foreskin. Circumcision was the visible sign and the mark of the covenant, and anyone who was not circumcised was cut off from Abraham's household and blessing. (see Genesis 17:1-14)

Within a year after this, Abraham's wife gave birth to their son, Isaac, just as God had promised. Isaac was the only heir to the covenant promises God had made to Abraham. When Isaac was a man, he had a son named Jacob, who was also the only heir to the covenant promises. During the course of his life, Jacob had twelve sons, and God changed Jacob's name to Israel. As Israel's sons' families grew and multiplied in number, they became known as the twelve tribes of Israel.

When there was famine in the land where they were still living in tents, Jacob/Israel moved his whole household down to Egypt, including his twelve sons and their families. At first, the people of Israel received favorable treatment with Pharaoh, the king and ruler of Egypt, and they settled in the fertile Egyptian territory of Goshen. But over time, the Israelites multiplied so much in number and blessing that the Egyptians thought it best to subject them to slavery so that they would not try to revolt or escape. Egypt became an iron-smelting furnace of affliction for the Israelites as the Egyptians set harsh taskmasters over them, forced them into slavery, afflicted them with heavy burdens and hard service, treated them ruthlessly, and made their lives very bitter. (see Exodus 1:1-14; Deuteronomy 4:20)

About four hundred years later, just as God had promised, God called upon a man named Moses (whose name means *to draw out*) to draw His people out of slavery so that they could freely worship Him. When Moses was unsure that anybody would listen to Him, God promised to confirm Moses as His servant with miracles, signs, and wonders that only the Creator of the Universe could orchestrate and that would bring judgment against all the gods of Egypt. So, God sent Moses to speak to the Hebrews and assure them that the time had come for Him to fulfill His promise to their ancestor Abraham. God also sent Moses to confront the most powerful man in the world, Pharaoh, to demand the release of His people, Israel, calling Israel His firstborn son. If Pharaoh would not agree to this, then God would kill Pharaoh's firstborn son. (see Exodus 4)

Unfortunately for him, Pharaoh was completely noncompliant with God's demand through Moses. Instead, Pharaoh hardened his heart and subjected the Israelites to even harsher slavery. Therefore, God worked mighty miracles and stretched out His hand to bring great plagues against the land and people of Egypt. Every time Pharaoh refused to let God's people go, God sent a plague. God turned the Nile river into blood, sent swarms of frogs, gnats, flies, caused the death of Egyptian livestock of anyone who did not listen and take cover, erupted boils and sores on Egyptian people and animals, rained down heavy hail mixed with fire, sent swarming locusts, and caused supernatural darkness over the land. Each plague unquestionably proved that the God of the Hebrews was more powerful than all the gods of Egypt. But Pharaoh exalted himself against God and still would not release the Hebrews from slavery after repeated requests and plagues. Therefore, the time for God's redemption of His people had come. God would fulfill His word by unleashing the destroyer to kill Pharaoh's firstborn son and all the firstborn sons in the entire land of Egypt.

Interestingly, during the course of these plagues, God made a distinction between His people and the Egyptians. The plagues did not affect the Hebrews or the territory of Goshen where they lived but only the Egyptians and their lands. God also made a way to protect and deliver His people from the destroyer.

These were the instructions God gave the Israelites through Moses for the first Passover. Anyone who desired to participate in the Passover was required to be circumcised. No foreigner was allowed to participate in Passover unless they had fully identified with God's people through the sign of God's covenant with Abraham. Then, on the tenth day of the month of Abib, each Israelite household was to take a lamb into their home. This lamb had to be a one-year-old male without any defects or blemishes. Then, at twilight on the fourteenth day of the month, they were to slaughter the lamb, drain its blood, and roast it over fire. Then, they were to paint the blood of the lamb over the doorposts of their homes and go inside, dressed and ready to leave Egypt at a moment's notice. God promised that wherever He saw the blood of the lamb, He would *pass over* the household so that the destroyer could not enter in or harm them. (see Exodus 12)

The Israelites believed God and did what Moses instructed them to do.

That night at midnight, God sent the destroyer to kill all the firstborn sons of Egypt. This plague struck every single household in Egypt that did not have the blood of the Passover lamb on its doorposts. Awakened by this horror and the cries of the people, Pharaoh finally commanded the Israelites to leave Egypt for fear that everyone in Egypt would wind up dead.

Then, God led His people out of Egypt by His presence in a pillar of cloud during the day and a pillar of fire at night. On the first day of their exodus, God led them to camp in the Egyptian wilderness. On the second day, God led them to camp at Pi-hahiroth, which means *mouth of the cavern*. Pi-hahiroth was located between Migdol and the Red Sea, and God told the Israelites to set up their camp facing Baal-zephon, which was the dwelling place of the Egyptian god Tsphon the Destroyer, an evil demon ruler. As spooky as this must have been, it also seemed to be a completely backwards route for the Hebrews to take since they were supposed to be headed for the Midianite wilderness to worship God and ultimately, the Promised Land.

Because of this, Pharaoh thought he could pursue the Israelites with horses and chariots, capture them, and enslave them again forever. So, Pharaoh and his armies charged in pursuit of the Israelites who appeared to be lost, hemmed in, and vulnerably stuck between the wilderness and the banks of the Red Sea. Even the Israelites started to think they had failed and would have been better off staying in Egypt. (see Exodus 14)

But through the night, God rolled away the waters of the Red Sea. The presence of the Lord, which had been going before the Hebrews, now shifted behind them to become their rear guard. All of the Israelites walked through the rolled away waters of the Red Sea on dry ground until they reached the other side. Pharaoh and the Egyptian army chased after them. But on the third day at daybreak, the waters returned to their place, engulfing the Egyptians, their horses, and chariots until none of them remained alive.

On that day, God saved Israel from their enemies and the oppression of slavery. From that day forward, they were no longer twelve tribes with a common ancestor. Now, they were a holy nation, created and birthed as God's very own people by God's mighty power through miracles, signs, and wonders. What started as one man who believed God had become a nation of that man's descendants who had been chosen before they were born to be special to Him.

The people of Israel had seen with their own eyes the mighty work of God on their behalf, so they sang songs of praise and worshiped God. And none of them were sick or feeble in any way.

For the full account of the original Passover, see Exodus 1-14. To read the songs of praise for God's work of redeeming His people, see Exodus 15, Psalm 105, and Psalms 113-118.

The Eternal Passover (the Reality)

The Passover we just described is a prophetic shadow for God's plan of redemption for all mankind. This plan began before the creation of the world when God selected His Son, Jesus, to be the eternal Passover Lamb and King of a people from all nations who would worship in God's presence for eternity.

> *1 Peter 1:20 - He was* ***chosen before the creation of the world,*** *but was revealed in these last times for your sake.*
>
> *Revelation 13:8b - the Lamb who was* ***slain from the creation of the world.***

Before mankind was even created, heaven's premier worship leader, Lucifer, threw a revolt against God in the heavens because He wanted to be in charge and have God's glory for himself. Therefore, he was thrown out of heaven with one third of the angels. (see Isaiah 14; Ezekiel 28; Revelation 12:9) Then, after God created mankind, the first man, Adam, and his wife, Eve, were tricked by the serpent into disobeying God. God had told them they would die if they ate from the tree of the knowledge of good and evil. But the serpent deceived them, and they ate it, thinking it would make them like God. Through this act of self-exaltation, they revealed that they were like the evil one in their hearts even though they had been created to be like God. As a consequence of their disobedience, they were banished from God's presence and from the tree of life, which would be guarded by mighty cherubim and a flaming sword from this point forward. (see Genesis 3) At this rate, the prospect of God's Son having a holy people who worshipped in God's presence seemed improbable at best.

To make matters worse, as soon as Adam and Eve ate from the forbidden tree, they sold themselves to the devil and were now his slaves with no hope of paying their way out. Additionally, for the first time since they had been created, they could perceive good from evil, which made it obvious that they were naked and this made them ashamed of themselves. Moreover, just as God had told them, the poison from the knowledge of good and evil caused their bodies to be subject to death and decay. On top of all of this, their lives became subjected to a curse of sweat and toil, strife, and the vanity and delusion of self-empowerment as they desperately longed to regain the paradise they had lost.

However, God made a promise that He would send a Savior to redeem all of the descendants of Adam and Eve from the devil's oppression, from sin, and from death by crushing the head of the evil one and even restoring Eden.

> *Genesis 3:14-15 - So the LORD God said to the serpent, "Because you have done this, "Cursed are you above all livestock and all wild animals! You will crawl on your belly and you will eat dust all the days of your life. And I will put enmity between you and the woman, and between your offspring and hers;* ***he will crush your head****, and you will strike his heel."*

A couple thousand years later, mankind was still in a sinful state, and the Savior God had promised to Adam and Eve had not yet been sent. This is when God called Abram/Abraham who believed that he had been selected by God to be the forefather of the Redeemer God had promised. (see John 8:56) Abraham was a descendant of Adam and Eve's son, Seth, and Noah's son, Shem, whom God had promised to bless. Then, Abraham had a son named Isaac, who had a son named Jacob, who is the one whose name God changed to Israel. One of Israel's son's names was Judah, and Judah's descendants led to David, who became the great King of Israel. David was a man after God's heart, and God promised David that one of his descendants would be the Messiah of Israel, and the Savior and Redeemer He had promised for mankind from the beginning. (see 2 Samuel 7)

When David was King, the people of Israel were the only nation on the face of the earth with a relationship with the one true God who created heaven and earth. They were also the only people on earth with God's

Law, which outlined His requirements of purity and righteousness, and God's Temple, which was situated at the one place on earth where God had chosen for acceptable sacrifices to be made to Him. God's Law required obedience to certain rules of conduct in order to maintain right standing with Him. Any offense against God's Law was counted as a spot or blemish on a person's record, and would cause the curse of the Law to go into effect. The curse of the Law detailed the schedule of punishments and includes incrementally increasing measures of every form of sickness and disease, mental illness, miscarriages and stillbirths, lack and oppression, war, and suppression by every kind of enemy. (see Deuteronomy 28; Leviticus 26) Spots and blemishes on anyone's record of conduct could only be washed away by the blood of a sacrifice offered to God in accordance with His regulations. While these regulations for blood sacrifices were carried out, the sins of the offender were transferred onto a sacrificial animal and then the animal died the death penalty in order to atone for their sin. After this, the requirements of justice were satisfied and the effects of the curse of the Law were brought to a halt.

About a thousand years after God's promise to David, it was time for God to send His Son. Like Abraham had left the splendors of Ur in order to dwell in tents, Jesus Christ left the majesty of heaven in order to dwell on earth as a man by being born into a tent of flesh. Jesus was born by the power of the Holy Spirit through a virgin named Mary. An angel of the Lord told Mary that the Holy Spirit would come upon her and she would conceive a Son whom she was to name Jesus, which means *salvation* or *God saves*, because He would save people from their sins. Mary's Son would be the Son of the Most High God, the promised descendant of King David who would rule and reign over an eternal Kingdom, and the Savior who would crush the head of the serpent just like God had promised to Adam and Eve back in the beginning. (see Luke 1) The King of the Universe was born in a feeding trough in Bethlehem, which certainly did not make Him appear to the eye to be the King of anything. Nevertheless, Jesus believed God.

Because Jesus was born by the power of the Holy Spirit, God was His Father, and He had the nature of God inside of Him even though He was born in a flesh like you and me and every other descendant of Adam and Eve. This is significant because Jesus lived His life in obedience to the nature of God within Him and not according the rebellious nature of Adam or, in other words, His flesh, making Him the only person in history who has ever been able to fulfill God's Law. From the day Jesus was born, through His childhood, adolescence, and into manhood, He never sinned. Therefore, He was completely unblemished and without defect in God's sight.

Then, the time came for Jesus to begin His earthly ministry and present Himself as God's Son, the Messiah of Israel, and the Savior of the world. As God had done for Moses, God confirmed Jesus as His chosen One through miracles, signs, and wonders so that people would believe God had sent Him and listen to Him. God sent His Son to speak to His people and tell them that the time had come for His Kingdom to be established, like He had promised to David. Also, like God sending Moses to confront Pharaoh, God sent Jesus to confront the god of this world, the devil, and demand the release of His people from the evil one's grip. (see 2 Corinthians 4:4; 1 John 5:19) Everywhere Jesus went, He healed the sick, cast out demons, raised the dead, multiplied food, and commanded the wind and the waves. Each miracle revealed that God had given Jesus power and authority over sin, sickness, the curse of the Law, demonic powers, and all of creation. These miracles unquestionably proved that God, the Father of Jesus, was far greater than the devil, the ancient serpent who had enslaved the descendants of Adam.

Unfortunately for them, the world rulers and the religious leaders did not consider or want Jesus to be their King. Like Pharaoh, with each miracle Jesus performed, they hardened their hearts all the more and sought a way to kill Him. Finally, the time came for God to bring about His masterpiece of redemption. From this point forward, God would make a distinction between those who believe Jesus and those who do not, and made a way for believers to be delivered from the evil one and all of his schemes.

On the tenth day of the month of Abib, the night when the Passover lamb was being selected, Jesus entered into Jerusalem. He rode in humbly on a donkey while the crowds shouted His praises, saying, "Hosanna in the

Highest to the Son of David!" This terribly upset the religious leaders and world rulers who continued to harden their hearts in rage against God and His Anointed One. Then, on the fourteenth day of the month, the night of Passover, at the one and only place in the world where sacrifices to God would be accepted, Jesus willingly offered His own life as the spotless eternal Passover Lamb of God.

> *Hebrews 10:5-7 - Therefore, when Christ came into the world, he said: "Sacrifice and offering you did not desire, but* ***a body you prepared for me****; with burnt offerings and sin offerings you were not pleased. Then I said,* ***'Here I am--it is written about me in the scroll-- I have come to do your will, my God.' "***

On the night of Passover, God released the destroyer against His own Firstborn Son. The devil entered into Judas who betrayed Jesus, and Jesus was arrested on false accusations and brought before the religious and world leaders. (see Luke 22; John 13:27) In the events that followed, Jesus was mocked, rejected, whipped, beaten, and slaughtered by men. His blood was poured out. Like the Passover Lamb that was roasted over fire, Jesus suffered the fiery wrath of God, which was unleashed in its fullness against Jesus on the cross until He was destroyed by death.

Jesus knew in advance that all of this must take place in order to fulfill God's purposes and promises to Him, and He laid down His life willingly because He believed that God would keep His word. (see John 10:17-18; Hebrews 12:2-3) This is because, while Jesus was being crucified, God was working a marvelous spiritual transaction and entering into a covenant with Jesus, the New Covenant, which was sealed with His blood for the forgiveness of our sins. As an unblemished blood sacrifice offered to God, all of the sins of mankind were laid upon Him on the cross and He took the punishment for all disobedience against God. As the Lamb of God, Jesus suffered the death penalty to atone for our sins dating all the way back to Adam's original sin.

> *Isaiah 53:4-12 - Surely* ***he took up our pain and bore our suffering****, yet we considered him punished by God, stricken by him, and afflicted. But* ***he was pierced for our transgressions, he was crushed for our iniquities; the punishment that brought us peace was on him, and by his wounds we are healed****. We all,*

> *like sheep, have gone astray, each of us has turned to our own way; and the LORD has laid on him the iniquity of us all. He was oppressed and afflicted, yet he did not open his mouth;* ***he was led like a lamb to the slaughter****, and as a sheep before its shearers is silent, so he did not open his mouth. By oppression and judgment he was taken away. Yet who of his generation protested? For he was* ***cut off from the land of the living; for the transgression of my people he was punished****. He was assigned a grave with the wicked, and with the rich in his death, though he had done no violence, nor was any deceit in his mouth. Yet it was the LORD's will to crush him and cause him to suffer, and though* ***the LORD makes his life an offering for sin****, he will see his offspring and prolong his days, and the will of the LORD will prosper in his hand. After he has suffered, he will see the light of life and be satisfied; by his knowledge my righteous servant will justify many, and* ***he will bear their iniquities****. Therefore I will give him a portion among the great, and he will divide the spoils with the strong, because he poured out his life unto death, and was numbered with the transgressors. For* ***he bore the sin of many****, and made intercession for the transgressors.*

Also, while Jesus suffered on the cross, the soul of every single human being in the history of mankind was drawn upon the cross with Him. (see John 12:32) This means that when Jesus was crucified, each of us were crucified with Him and when He died and was buried, we died and were buried with Him. (see Galatians 2:20; Romans 6:4-8; Colossians 3:3)

When Jesus died, He committed His Spirit, the Holy Spirit, into the hands of God. His Spirit ascended to heaven, and His soul descended down to the pit of Hell—the eternal fiery inferno and domain of the devil. (see Luke 23:46; 2 Corinthians 5:8) On the second day, His body laid in the grave, a cavernous tomb. From a natural standpoint, this all seemed completely backwards to the way we would expect the King of the Universe to take. Even Jesus' disciples felt defeated, humiliated, and ashamed because they had believed Jesus was God's Messiah, but now He was dead. They did not understand what God was doing, and everything seemed utterly hopeless. Not to mention that we know for a fact that the forces of evil thought they had victoriously conquered Jesus once and for all because if they had known what God was about to do, they would never have crucified Him. (1 Corinthians 2:8)

But on the third day, God sent the Spirit of Holiness from heaven to the pit of Hell to rescue and deliver His Son out of death. (see Romans 1:4) The devil and his servants tried to seize Him forever, but the powers of Hell did not prevail against Him. (see Matthew 16:18) Jesus' Spirit and soul returned to His body and quickened it to life, transforming it from a perishable body into an incorruptible resurrection body by the power of God. (see 1 Corinthians 15) Like the parted waters of the Red Sea, God rolled away the stone that covered Jesus' grave, and He walked out of the tomb.

Through Jesus' sacrifice and resurrection, God saved His eternal people from sin, the curse of the Law, and every oppression of the evil one, including sickness and death. Now that the requirements of justice have been satisfied, everyone who believes in the blood of Jesus as our eternal Passover Lamb has perfect righteousness with God as if we have never sinned.

This is because when Jesus was raised from the dead, we who believe were included in His resurrection. (see Colossians 2:12) What appeared to be just one man was actually millions of souls from every age of history who were chosen before the creation of the world to be God's children. (see Ephesians 1:5, 11) Like Israel was redeemed out of the furnace of affliction and transformed from twelve tribes into one holy nation, we have been redeemed out of death and eternal condemnation, and changed from descendants of Adam from every nation, tribe, and tongue into a new generation of humanity. (see Revelation 5:9) We have been born again through the resurrection of Jesus by the power of God to be His beloved children. (see John 3:6-8; 1 Peter 1:3, 23)

Moreover, like the Egyptian armies that pursued the Israelites, all of our sins and everything about our inherited Adamic nature have been put to death and cast into the bottom of the sea. Jesus conquered the enemies of mankind and crushed the head of the serpent! Hallelujah! Let us worship and sing the praises of our King!

The Blood of the Lamb

In the original Passover, the Law of God had not yet been given to the Israelites. Therefore, at the time of the Passover, they were not yet responsible for upholding God's standard of righteousness and purity in order to receive God's blessings. Their deliverance was based entirely on the blood of the lamb. For us as followers of Jesus, because Jesus fulfilled the Law and set us free from it, we are not required to meet the demands of the Law in order to have right standing with God. Jesus did not negate the Law of God for us through His blood but rather, He fulfilled it on our behalf so that we can receive the benefits of God's forgiveness and the blessings merited only by those who have a clean record before God. (see Romans 3:25-26) This means that health and healing are ours to receive freely as we trust exclusively in the blood of Jesus, our Passover Lamb, and not in our own merits.

Under the Law, at the Temple of God, when people brought their prescribed blood sacrifices of bulls, sheep, goats, or birds, they brought the greatest sacrifice they could afford to bring. (see Leviticus 5:7, 14:21) A blood sacrifice of equal or greater value than the offense incurred must be offered. For example, in God's regulations of offenses between people, the standard of payment was an eye for an eye, tooth for tooth, hand for hand, and foot for foot. (see Exodus 21:24) When an offering was brought to God, all the sins of the person bringing the offering were transferred onto their sacrificial animal. Then, the animal was presented to God to shed its blood and give its life in the place of the person who had sinned so that the person could continue to live and be blessed as if they had never sinned at all.

> *Hebrews 9:22 - In fact, the law requires that nearly everything be cleansed with blood, and* ***without the shedding of blood there is no forgiveness****.*

> *Leviticus 17:11 - For* ***the life of a creature is in the blood****, and I have given it to you to make atonement for yourselves on the altar;* ***it is the blood that makes atonement for one's life****.*

Accordingly, in order for God's terms of payment for the forgiveness of every sin of every person since Adam to be satisfied, a sacrifice of infinite worth was required. The Good News is that because of God's great love for mankind, He who is the owner of all creation gave the best offering He could afford to give by giving His one and only Son.

> *John 3:16-17 - For* ***God so loved the world that he gave his one and only Son****, that whoever believes in him shall not perish but have eternal life. For God did not send his Son into the world to condemn the world, but to save the world through him.*

One drop of the blood of God's perfect Son is more valuable in God's sight than millions of bulls, sheep, goats, and birds. Because of this, we can be fully assured that Jesus' sacrifice is completely sufficient to pay for all of our sins and errors.

> *Hebrews 10:8-10, 14 - First he said, "Sacrifices and offerings, burnt offerings and sin offerings you did not desire, nor were you pleased with them"--though they were offered in accordance with the law. Then he said, "Here I am, I have come to do your will." He sets aside the first to establish the second. And by that will,* ***we have been made holy through the sacrifice of the body of Jesus Christ once for all****. ... For* ***by one sacrifice he has made perfect forever those who are being made holy****.*

This means that we can continue to live and be blessed as if we had never sinned at all because all of our sins were laid upon Jesus.

Additionally, through His sacrifice and resurrection, Jesus set us free from the Law. Therefore, we are no longer subject to rules and regulations for earning or meriting right standing with God or any of His blessings. This is significant as we examine the work of Jesus pertaining to healing because trusting in the blood of the lamb is entirely an act of faith in God's ability to fulfill what He has promised. As an act of faith, it is only effective for those who put it to use. For example, any Hebrew who did not paint the blood of the lamb over their doorpost would have awoken to discover that the destroyer had been allowed to have his way in their home. It had nothing to do with what good or bad things they may have been doing behind their door. The only thing that was relevant in God's sight was whether or not they had painted the blood of the lamb on their door. Similarly, any of us who have placed our faith entirely in the blood of Jesus and not our own merits will be able to receive our healing from God as a free gift, by grace through faith. It has nothing to do with what we deserve based on the good or bad things we have done because the only thing that is relevant in God's sight is whether or not we believe in the sufficiency of the shed blood of His Son, Jesus, our Passover Lamb.

Redemption of the Firstborn Son

The *firstborn son* represents the power of a man or father to produce heirs and future generations. (see Genesis 49:3) Firstborn sons are considered a blessing from God, become the head of their father's family, receive a double portion of inheritance, and are especially blessed. To *redeem* something means to pay the price required to purchase it and restore it to its rightful owner.

Leading up to the first Passover, God redeemed Israel, His firstborn son. (see Exodus 4:22) When God purchased His people out of Egyptian slavery, He did so at the expense of the firstborn sons of the Egyptians who were destroyed by the destroyer. From this point forward as an act of remembrance of the price that was paid for their redemption, all the firstborn sons of Israel were required to be offered to God and consecrated for His purposes. The life of the firstborn belonged to God. However, rather than literally surrendering their firstborn sons on the altar of sacrifice, an animal was sacrificed in the son's place to acknowledge that he was totally dedicated to God. (see Exodus 13:1, 11-16) As a side note, Mary consecrated Jesus to God in this way. (see Luke 2:22-24)

In the eternal Passover, God made a way to redeem the descendants of His son, Adam. (see Luke 3:38) When God purchased for Himself a people from every nation, tribe, and tongue to be His children, He did so at the expense of Jesus, His one and only begotten Son (meaning that He was literally born as God's Son), who was destroyed by God's wrath and death on a cross. This means that all of us who believe Jesus are consecrated to God as His beloved children and as the congregation of the firstborn. We have been made brothers and sisters of Jesus so that we can offer our lives as living sacrifices to live for God and His purposes the way Jesus did when He was in a flesh like ours. We have been bought with a price and our lives belong to God.

Hebrews 12:23 NLT - You have come to the ***assembly of God's firstborn children****, whose names are written in heaven. You have come to God Himself, who is the judge over all things. You have come to the spirits of the righteous ones in heaven who have now been made perfect.*

1 Peter 1:3-4a - Praise be to the God and Father of our Lord Jesus Christ! In His great mercy He has given us ***new birth*** *into a living hope through the resurrection of Jesus Christ from the dead, and into an inheritance that can never perish, spoil or fade.*

Romans 8:29 - For those God foreknew He also predestined to be conformed to the image of His Son, that ***He might be the firstborn among many brothers and sisters****.*

Through this whole process, Jesus as God's Firstborn Son paid the price for our redemption by selling Himself to the devil. Therefore, when God purchased Jesus back from the evil one, He did so at the expense of everyone descended from His son Adam who refuses to believe Jesus and who will be ultimately destroyed in the fires of hell. God begot Jesus again as His one and only Son and the Firstborn from the dead. Jesus is consecrated to God as the only Savior of mankind.

Colossians 1:18 - And He is the head of the body, the church; He is the beginning and the ***firstborn from among the dead****, so that in everything He might have the supremacy.*

Since this covers a lot of firstborn sons and a lot of redemption prices being paid, here is a quick reference chart to help you see it more clearly.

Redeemed	Cost of Redemption
Israel, God's firstborn son	Firstborn sons of Egypt
Believers in Jesus. Children of God. Assembly of the firstborn.	Jesus, God's Firstborn Son
Jesus, Firstborn from the Dead	Sons/descendants of God's son, Adam, who reject Jesus.

Interestingly, Israel was purchased by God as a nation without sickness or feebleness, as if they had never been oppressed by slave masters. God made a distinction between His people and those who were not His, and one of the defining marks of this was the lack of plagues and disease. Similarly, when Jesus purchased our redemption so that we can be God's children, He paid the price for us to be free from sin and its effects, including every sickness, as if we were not descendants of Adam, the original sinner. Even though our earthly Adamic bodies will eventually die, in the meantime, as sons and daughters of God, healing from all the diseases of this world was included in the price paid for us through the sacrifice of God's Firstborn Son, Jesus Christ. Plus, someday we will receive an imperishable resurrection body to last for all eternity. Hallelujah!

A Chosen Generation

In the first Passover, Israel was created as a new nation and taken by God out of the nation of Egypt.

> *Deuteronomy 4:34-35 - Has any god ever tried to* ***take for himself one nation out of another nation****, by testings, by signs and wonders, by war, by a mighty hand and an outstretched arm, or by great and awesome deeds, like all the things the LORD your God did for you in Egypt before your very eyes? You were shown these things so that you might know that the LORD is God; besides him there is no other.*

Since Israel's birth as a nation, there have been two kinds of nations on the earth in God's sight: Israel and all the other nations or, you could say, Jews and non-Jews. Starting in the days of Abraham, Hebrews were the only people on earth with a covenant relationship with the one true God, Creator of heaven and earth. Accordingly, anyone from any other nation who wanted to enter into relationship with the Most High God was required to be circumcised and convert to Judaism. God made no other way.

In the eternal Passover, a new generation of humanity was created out of an existing generation of humanity. God created a new type of man from the descendants of Adam through the resurrection of Jesus. The first generation of man, including all the descendants of Adam, are part of an evil, adulterous, and faithless generation that is doomed to eternal condemnation as sons of disobedience and offspring of the devil. (see Matthew 12:39; John 8:44; Matthew 16:23; Mark 9:19; Luke 11:50-51) If this offends you, note that humankind proved this to be true when we killed the Son of God. (see Isaiah 53:6, 8) The second generation of man was created through the resurrection of Jesus and includes everyone from every age who believes that Jesus is Lord. We are the people that God promised to Jesus as His inheritance, the ones who will worship God for all eternity. We are His offspring and a generation that had not been born until Jesus' resurrection. (see Isaiah 53:10; Psalm 22:30-31) We are a chosen generation and a new form of humanity.

> *1 Peter 2:9 NKJV - But you [are] a* ***chosen generation, a royal priesthood, a holy nation, His own special people****, that you may proclaim the praises of Him who called you out of darkness into His marvelous light;*
>
> *Ephesians 2:11-16 - Therefore, remember that formerly you who are Gentiles by birth and called "uncircumcised" by those who call themselves "the circumcision" (which is done in the body by human hands)-- remember that at that time you were separate from Christ, excluded from citizenship in Israel and foreigners to the covenants of the promise, without hope and without God in the world. But now in Christ Jesus you who once were far away have been brought near by the blood of Christ. For He Himself is our peace, who has made the two groups one and has destroyed the barrier, the dividing wall of hostility, by setting aside in His flesh the law with its commands and regulations. His purpose was to create in Himself one* ***new humanity*** *out of the two, thus making peace, and in one body to reconcile both of them to God through the cross, by which He put to death their hostility.*

This means that now there are only two kinds of people on the earth because there are two generations of man. Anyone from the first generation of man who wants to be included in God's eternal covenant and blessings has to confess with their mouth that Jesus is Lord and believe in their heart that God raised Him from the dead. The one true God who created heaven and earth has made no other way to be saved.

In addition to this, after Jesus proved that He had been raised from the dead, He ascended to heaven and sat down at the right hand of God. Just like we who believe were included in His resurrection, we also ascended with Him and are seated in heavenly places as citizens of heaven even though we still live in bodies here on earth. (see Ephesians 1:3, 2:6; Philippians 3:20) To assure us that we have been included in the new generation of mankind as God's children, after Jesus ascended to heaven, He poured out the Holy Spirit into the hearts of everyone who believes in Him. (see Acts 2:33) It is the Holy Spirit dwelling within us that enables us to cry out to God as our Father.

> *Romans 8:15 - The Spirit you received does not make you slaves, so that you live in fear again; rather,* ***the Spirit you received brought about your adoption to sonship. And by Him we cry, "Abba, Father."***

> *Galatians 4:6 -* ***Because you are His sons, God sent the Spirit of His Son into our hearts****, the Spirit who calls out, "****Abba, Father****."*

We have become children of God who have His divine nature inside of us. We have become a new creation that was designed by God to function the same way Jesus did when He was on earth. The same Holy Spirit that directed and empowered Jesus when He lived in a flesh like ours is now dwelling inside of us to enable us to live as a new creation.

> *2 Corinthians 5:17 - Therefore, if anyone is in Christ, the* ***new creation*** *has come: The old has gone, the new is here!*

> *2 Peter 1:3-4 - His divine power has given us everything we need for a godly life through our knowledge of Him who called us by His own glory and goodness. Through these He has given us His very great and precious promises, so that through them you may* ***participate in the divine nature****, having escaped the corruption in the world caused by evil desires.*

> *Galatians 6:15 - Neither circumcision nor uncircumcision means anything; what counts is the* ***new creation****.*

As a Son of God, Jesus was never sick. His perfect record of righteousness never permitted any sickness to touch Him and the Holy Spirit supplied the life-giving power of God to His mortal body. Now for us, because we receive the righteousness of Jesus as a free gift through faith in Him, sickness has no right to touch us. Plus, we have the Holy Spirit within us to give life to our mortal bodies, healing us and keeping us in health according to our faith in Jesus.

Inclusion in the Covenant

In the first Passover, circumcision was the visible, outward sign of inclusion in God's covenant promises to Abraham. No Israelites or foreigners were allowed to participate in the Passover unless they were circumcised into the covenant. (see Exodus 12:43-49) Then, when the Israelites literally walked through the rolled-away waters of the Red Sea, they were figuratively baptized into Moses and included in the nation of Israel while their enemies were buried in the sea. (see 1 Corinthians 10:1-2) God's presence in the pillar of cloud by day and the pillar of fire by night led the way for everyone included in the original Passover.

In the eternal Passover, when we first place our faith in the blood of Jesus, we are marked and sealed by the Holy Spirit and set apart from the rest of the world as one of God's children. (see Ephesians 1:13; 1 John 4:13-15) This is a spiritual circumcision of our hearts as God rolls away our Adamic hearts of stone, sin, and disobedience and replaces them with the tender heart of Jesus. (see Romans 2:29; Jeremiah 31:33-34; Ezekiel 36:26) When we are baptized in water, we outwardly display the inward change that has taken place in our hearts. As we are literally submerged into the waters of baptism, we are figuratively including ourselves in the death of Jesus, putting to death the sinful nature we inherited from Adam and washing away all of our sins. As we are raised up out of the waters of baptism, we signify our participation in the resurrection of Jesus and in the New Covenant as those who are righteous in God's sight as if we had never sinned. Our old life is rolled away and we emerge as a new creation and a child of God.

> *Colossians 2:11-12 - In Him you were also circumcised with a circumcision not performed by human hands.* ***Your whole self***

> ***ruled by the flesh was put off when you were circumcised by Christ****, having been buried with Him in baptism, in which you were also raised with Him through your faith in the working of God, who raised Him from the dead. (see also Romans 6:3)*
>
> *Philippians 3:3 - For it is* ***we who are the circumcision****, we who serve God by His Spirit, who boast in Christ Jesus, and who put no confidence in the flesh...*

The Holy Spirit is God's presence with us that guides us on the path God has planned for our lives. The Holy Spirit also reminds us that our enemies have been conquered through the sacrifice of Jesus so that we can live as those who have a clean record before God because our former way of life has been buried forever in the grave.

> *Colossians 1:21-23a - Once you were alienated from God and were enemies in your minds because of your evil behavior. But now He has reconciled you by Christ's physical body through death* ***to present you holy in His sight, without blemish and free from accusation****-- if you continue in your faith, established and firm, and do not move from the hope held out in the Gospel.*

All of this is to say that by our faith, revealed by our baptism in water, we have been included in God's covenant with Jesus. This means that we are now positioned to receive ALL of God's benefits and blessings. These blessings include healing for all of our diseases. Under the Old Covenant, God's natural, earthly blessings for His people includes healing for all diseases. (see Deuteronomy 28:1-14; Psalm 103:3) Even more so in the New Covenant, God's spiritual blessings include every gift of heaven available to us right now as we trust in Jesus. There is no sickness in heaven. (see Ephesians 1:3)

The Worship of a Redeemed People

After the first Passover when the Israelites saw the destruction of their enemies, they worshipped God and sang songs of praise at the banks of the Red Sea. In our eternal Passover, when we understand what God has done for us by sending Jesus to conquer our eternal enemies of sin and death, the only proper response is to offer our lives to Him as an act of worship.

Romans 12:1 - Therefore, I urge you, brothers and sisters, in view of God's mercy, to ***offer your bodies as a living sacrifice,*** *holy and pleasing to God--****this is your true and proper worship***.

Interestingly, this verse does not say to offer God our hearts, our souls, or our minds but instead our *bodies*. This does not mean that we literally place our bodies on an altar of sacrifice, but that we offer every part of ourselves to live for God and His Kingdom, including trusting Him with our bodies. Through the blood of our eternal Passover Lamb, Jesus, we triumph over sin, sickness, and all the devil's schemes because even death has lost its power to threaten us.

Revelation 12:11 - They ***triumphed over him [the evil one] by the blood of the Lamb*** *and by the word of their testimony; they* ***did not love their lives so much as to shrink from death***.

This said, just like the newborn nation of Israel had other ferocious enemies that sought to attack and destroy them, we as born-again believers still have enemies in this world that seek to ensnare and defeat us. Our biggest remaining enemy is our own unbelief in what Jesus has done for us in addition to the lies of the evil one which attempt to persuade us to doubt that the redemption price for the forgiveness of our sins and for our healing has been paid in full through the sacrifice of Jesus.

Therefore, the only work left for us to do is to worship God and rejoice in all that Jesus has done for us. We do this when we believe that He has redeemed us as firstborn sons and daughters of God to be unique among all people of the earth as a chosen generation. We do this when we place our lives in His hands and trust Him to save, heal, and deliver us as we spiritually paint the blood of Jesus over the doorposts of our hearts as our eternal Passover Lamb. When we do this, we will reveal God's will on earth as it is in heaven where there is no sickness, crying, or pain and we will reveal God's goodness, power, and love to the rest of the world.

Chapter Two

DELIVERED & TRANSFERRED

After the Israelites walked through the waters of the Red Sea, they turned around to see with their own eyes the destruction of their enemies. God had delivered His people from slavery, oppression, and subjugation to evil authority and had transferred them to safety in the wilderness where they could worship Him freely. For us as followers of Jesus, as we believe God for healing, we must perceive accurately that our enemies have been just as conquered as Pharaoh and the Egyptian army were for the Israelites. Through our inclusion in the death and resurrection of Jesus, we have been delivered by God from the causes of sickness and transferred to a place of safety and blessing as His children.

> *Colossians 1:13-14 ESV - He has* ***delivered us from the domain of darkness*** *and* ***transferred us to the kingdom of His beloved Son****, in whom we have redemption, the forgiveness of sins.*

Even though the world comes up with all sorts of reasons for sickness and disease, the Word of God is the only authoritative source of truth about everything. According to the Scriptures, there are only three reasons for sickness: sin, the curse of the Law, and the devil. These are the enemies of mankind which were defeated through the death and resurrection of Jesus so that by faith, we can be free from their effects in our life, including sickness.

> *Colossians 2:13-15 - When you were dead in your sins and in the uncircumcision of your flesh, God made you alive with Christ. He* ***forgave us all our sins****, having* ***canceled the charge of our legal indebtedness, which stood against us and condemned us****; He has taken it away, nailing it to the cross. And having* ***disarmed the powers and authorities****, He made a public spectacle of them,* ***triumphing over them by the cross****.*

Even though we are identifying sin, the curse, and the devil as the

Biblical causes of sickness, it is worth noting that Jesus never went digging into or exposing people's sins before healing them. Therefore, as you read this chapter, please do not start looking at yourself or any other sick person with a condemning eye of accusation. With full knowledge of the root reason for their illness, Jesus looked upon the sick with mercy, not counting their sins against them. The objective of this chapter is not only to gain a Biblical perspective on the causes of sickness but also to reveal how Jesus overcame each one of these causes on our behalf. We are not healed because these reasons for sickness do not exist. We are healed by grace through faith when we believe that Jesus dealt with and triumphed over these causes at the cross.

Sickness Due to Sin

Sickness was never God's will for mankind in the first place. There was no sickness or death in the Garden of Eden. But when Adam and Eve believed the serpent and ate from the tree of the knowledge of good and evil, sin and death began to reign over us. God told them in advance that the consequence for eating from the wrong tree would be that they would surely die. This word for *die* in Hebrew means *to die prematurely or to be worthy of death.* Although this word can indicate instantaneous death, and there are Biblical examples of this, it is also the same expression that would be used for gradual but unavoidable death. After their disobedience, Adam and Eve were cut off from God, the source of life, and therefore, sickness and death became inevitable. From this point forward, instead of everlasting health and life with God, every descendant of Adam will surely die.

> *Romans 5:12-14 - Therefore, just as* ***sin entered the world through one man, and death through sin, and in this way death came to all people, because all sinned****-- To be sure, sin was in the world before the law was given, but sin is not charged against anyone's account where there is no law. Nevertheless,* ***death reigned from the time of Adam*** *to the time of Moses,* ***even over those who did not sin by breaking a command, as did Adam****, who is a pattern of the one to come.*

There are several examples in the Scriptures of illnesses between the time of Adam's fall and the time the Law was given to God's people through Moses. Around the days of Noah, God grew weary of contending with sinful man and shortened the lifespan of people to 120 years. (see Genesis 6:3) When Abraham and his wife, Sarah, went down to Egypt, Pharaoh was struck with serious diseases for taking Sarah into his palace. (see Genesis 12:10-20) The first supernatural healing in the Scriptures took place in a very similar encounter between Abraham and Abimelech, the king of Gerar. While Sarah was in Abimelech's custody, Abimelech's wife and every woman in his household was struck barren with infertility. The women were healed only after Sarah was returned to Abraham untouched, and when Abraham prayed to God for their wombs to be opened. (see Genesis 20) Two of Judah's sons were struck with instantaneous death on account of their wickedness. (see Genesis 38:7, 10) The men of Shechem were deceived into circumcising themselves and suffered pain and soreness for several days. (see Genesis 34) Isaac's eyesight and Jacob's health both declined rapidly toward the end of their lives. (see Genesis 27:1, 48:1) Even though this seems obvious enough, consider that God's will for us is to have strength and vigor equal to our days and even pain in our bodies was never His will for us. To give a contrast, Abraham and Moses fulfilled their 120 years of life with undiminished vitality and Caleb was as strong and ready for battle at 85 years old as he had been at age 45. (see Genesis 25:7-8; Deuteronomy 34:7; Joshua 14:10-11)

While the Israelites were in Egypt for four hundred years, they suffered from the same diseases the Egyptians had. (see Deuteronomy 7:15) Somewhere in the course of the Passover events, they were healed from all of these diseases in addition to being supernaturally protected from the plagues that struck Egypt. Moreover, within a few days of their exodus from Egypt, God promised to keep them free from sickness, disease, and infirmity if they would simply obey His voice and do what He told them to do. (see Exodus 15:26) Then, when God gave the Law to His people, He clearly articulated His commands, statutes, rules, and regulations for how to behave righteously. The Law plainly states that health and freedom from disease are rewards for obedience. According to the Law, choosing to obey God is the only way to earn and maintain a long healthy life.

Exodus 23:25-26 - Worship the LORD your God, and His blessing will be on your food and water. ***I will take away sickness from among you, and none will miscarry or be barren*** *in your land.* ***I will give you a full life span.***

Deuteronomy 7:12, 14-15 - If you pay attention to these laws and are careful to follow them, then the LORD your God will keep His covenant of love with you, as He swore to your ancestors. ... You will be blessed more than any other people; ***none of your men or women will be childless****, nor will any of your livestock be without young.* ***The LORD will keep you free from every disease. He will not inflict on you the horrible diseases you knew in Egypt****, but He will inflict them on all who hate you.*

Deuteronomy 32:46-47 - He said to them, "Take to heart all the words I have solemnly declared to you this day, so that you may command your children to obey carefully all the words of this law. ***They are not just idle words for you--they are your life. By them you will live long*** *in the land you are crossing the Jordan to possess."*

Deuteronomy 30:19-20 NLT - "Today I have given you the ***choice between life and death****, between blessings and curses. Now I call on heaven and earth to witness the choice you make. Oh, that you would* ***choose life****, so that you and your descendants might live!* ***You can make this choice by loving the LORD your God, obeying Him, and committing yourself firmly to Him. This is the key to your life****. And if you love and obey the LORD, you will live long in the land the LORD swore to give your ancestors Abraham, Isaac, and Jacob."*

The bottom line of all of this is that obedience to God leads to health and life. Based on this, in the event that people became sick, it was an indication that they had disobeyed God and had sin in their life. According to the Law and as we covered in the last chapter, the only way for them to be restored to right standing with God in order to be healed was to offer the required blood sacrifice to pay for their sin.

Unfortunately, nobody in the history of mankind has been able to live in perfect obedience in order to fulfill God's Law from the heart in the way that He intended it to be lived out. Not one person has ever been able to attain righteousness before God on their own merits and therefore, nobody has had the legal right to perpetual health and eternal life. That is, nobody except Jesus. When Jesus was born in flesh like ours with the nature of God within Him, He lived the perfectly obedient life with no error or deviation even in His motives and attitudes. He lived His life in accordance with God's perfect standard and maintained righteousness at all times. (see Matthew 5:17; Hebrews 4:15) Therefore, only Jesus sustained right standing with God, and only Jesus is entitled to all of God's blessings, including divinely maintained health and life.

During His earthly ministry, Jesus affirmed that obedience to God's Law is the only way to earn God's blessings and eternal life. (see Luke 10:25-28, 18:18-19) Moreover, He raised the standard of obedience to one that calls into account the motives of the heart and not just outward religious talk and behavior. (see Matthew 5-7) Additionally, because Jesus' disciples knew the Law, they plainly recognized sin and sin passed down through generations as a cause of sickness. (see John 9:2) Jesus also made a direct connection between healing and the forgiveness of sin. For example, when a paralyzed man was brought to Jesus, Jesus healed him by forgiving his sins.

> *Matthew 9:2 - Some men brought to Him a paralyzed man, lying on a mat. When Jesus saw their faith, He said to the man, "Take heart, son;* ***your sins are forgiven.****"*

This man was healed, stood up, and walked home. Of course, this terribly upset the religious leaders who knew that the requirement for forgiveness of sins was a blood sacrifice. They did not understand what Jesus was doing or what He was about to do.

Instead of keeping His right standing with God and all of its blessings to Himself, Jesus offered Himself to God as an unblemished sacrifice on our behalf. When Jesus was on the cross as an offering for our sin, all of our transgressions and iniquities were laid upon Him. Transgressions include everything we have done wrong in rebellion against God's perfect standard, all of our trespasses off the narrow path of life, and everything we have willingly or unknowingly participated in that is forbidden by God and deserves to be punished. Iniquities include the perversity and depravity of our hearts, our hidden faults, failures, and mischievous thoughts, and any guilt that we have contracted by sinning. All of these things were imputed onto Jesus, charging Him with our record of sin. Through this, He became sin even though He had never sinned. He fulfilled not only perfect obedience to God's standard of conduct to maintain right standing with God but also fulfilled God's sacrificial requirements so that our sins could be forgiven.

> *Isaiah 53:5-6, 10-11 - But He was pierced **for our transgressions**, He was crushed **for our iniquities**; the punishment that brought us peace was on Him, and by His wounds we are healed. We all, like sheep, have gone astray, each of us has turned to our own way; and the LORD has **laid on Him the iniquity of us all**. ... Yet it was the LORD's will to crush Him and cause Him to suffer, and though the LORD **makes His life an offering for sin**, He will see his offspring and prolong His days, and the will of the LORD will prosper in His hand. After He has suffered, He will see the light of life and be satisfied; by His knowledge my righteous servant will justify many, and **He will bear their iniquities**.*

> *1 Peter 3:18a - For Christ also **suffered once for sins**, the righteous for the unrighteous, to bring you to God.*

> *2 Corinthians 5:21 - **God made Him who had no sin to be sin for us**, so that in Him we might become the righteousness of God.*

> *Romans 3:25-26 - **God presented Christ as a sacrifice of atonement**, through the shedding of His blood--to be received by faith. He did this to demonstrate His righteousness, because in His forbearance He had left the sins committed beforehand unpunished-- He did it to demonstrate His righteousness at the present time, so as to be just and the one who justifies those who have faith in Jesus.*

> *1 John 2:2 - **He is the atoning sacrifice for our sins**, and not only for ours but also **for the sins of the whole world**.*

Therefore, because all of our sins were placed upon Jesus, we receive a perfect record before God as if we had never sinned. This means that we can have a totally clear conscience before God because, in His sight, we are holy and blameless and we can freely receive the benefits of those who have right standing with Him, including health and healing.

> *1 John 1:7 - But if we walk in the light, as He is in the light, we have fellowship with one another, and* ***the blood of Jesus, His Son, purifies us from all sin****.*

> *Ephesians 1:7 - In Him we have redemption* ***through his blood, the forgiveness of sins****, in accordance with the riches of God's grace...*

> *Colossians 1:22 - But now He has reconciled you by Christ's physical body through death* ***to present you holy in His sight, without blemish and free from accusation****...*

> *Hebrews 10:14 - For* ***by one sacrifice He has made perfect*** *forever those who are being made holy.*

> *Hebrews 9:14 - How much more, then, will* ***the blood of Christ****, who through the eternal Spirit offered Himself unblemished to God,* ***cleanse our consciences*** *from acts that lead to death, so that we may serve the living God!*

This means that by faith in what Jesus has done for us, we can live freed from sin and be as blessed as the One who never disobeyed God. Like a sinner who has offered a sacrifice of high enough value to pay the price for our sin, we can go on with our lives as those who have been restored to the place of life and blessing. Like the paralyzed man who was healed when Jesus forgave His sins, we can get up, be healed, and live as those who have been forgiven. Even though our Adamic bodies will still die because of Adam's original sin, we can have perpetual health and strength until the day we die as a blessing and privilege of those who have right standing with God.

Sickness As a Result of the Curse of the Law

In the same way that obeying God results in blessing, disobeying God results in being cursed. Essentially, a curse is a declaration or mandate of a negative outcome in someone's life and is typically warranted because of something they have done. For example, after Adam and Eve disobeyed God in Eden, mankind was cursed to a life of sweat and toil, pain in childbirth, and the ground was cursed to produce thorns and thistles in order to make Adam's cursed life even more miserable. The serpent was also cursed to crawl on the ground and would eventually be trampled by one of Adam and Eve's descendants. (see Genesis 3) After Cain killed his brother Abel, he was cursed to be a wanderer and bear a mark that prevented anyone from killing him so as to put him out of his misery. (see Genesis 4:11-12) Noah's grandson, Canaan, was cursed to lowliness and subjugated servitude after his father, Ham, dishonored Noah. (see Genesis 9:24-25) Anyone who curses God's people will be cursed in return. (see Genesis 12:3) All of these curses were put into place before the Law of God was given, and there are other similar spoken curses throughout the Scriptures.

This said, when God gave His Law to His people, it included the schedule of punishment for disobedience—the Curse of the Law. This goes into effect when God remembers sin, which means that He calls it to account. The Curse of the Law is written out in Leviticus 26 and Deuteronomy 28. These chapters make it clear that illnesses not specifically mentioned by name are included in the Curse of the Law and that repeated and ongoing disobedience or rebellion will be penalized from generation to generation with incremental seven-fold increases in the severity of the prescribed afflictions. I encourage you to read both of these chapters thoroughly to gain insight into the Curse of the Law. However, for the sake of our study, I will pull out some of the highlights that pertain to our physical and mental health and well-being.

Leviticus 26	
v. 16	Sudden terror, wasting disease, and fever that destroys your sight and saps your strength.
v. 20	Your strength spent in vain.
v. 22	Wild animals eat your children.
v. 23	Sword, plagues, enemies.
v. 36	Fearful hearts.
v. 38-39	Death. Devoured by enemies. Waste away.

Deuteronomy 28	
v. 18	Cursed womb.
v. 20	Confusion and rebuke in everything you do until you are destroyed and come to sudden ruin.
v. 21	Plagues and diseases until you are destroyed.
v. 22	Wasting disease, fever, inflammation, scorching heat, drought, blight, mildew, plagues.
v. 25, 37	Defeat by enemies, become an object of horror.
v. 26	Your dead carcasses will be food for the birds and wild animals.
v. 27	Boils, tumors, festering sores, and itch which cannot be cured.
v. 28, 34	Madness, blindness, confusion of mind.
v. 32	Powerlessness, no one to help.
v. 35	Painful boils on knees and legs that cannot be cured, spreading from the soles of your feet to the top of your head.
v. 59	Fearful plagues, harsh and prolonged disasters, severe and lingering illnesses.
v. 60	All of the diseases and plagues that you dread will cling to you.
v. 61	Every kind of sickness and disaster not recorded in this Book of the Law, until you are destroyed.
v. 65	No rest, anxious mind, eyes weary with longing, despairing heart.
v. 66	Constant suspense, filled with dread, never sure of your life.

Based on this, when someone became ill, it was typically presumed that they were being punished by God for something they or their ancestors had done. Their sickness was regarded as justice being served in their life because they were getting what they rightfully deserved.

In Jesus' day, many people approached Him for healing by crying out, "Have mercy on me!" Through this simple statement, they were asking Jesus to use His God-given authority to pardon them and not give them what they deserved. They knew and did not deny that they deserved the

Curse of the Law and all of the afflictions, diseases, and maladies it included and they begged to not suffer the punishment their sin warranted. Jesus healed them, releasing them from the Curse of the Law.

But again, this pardon was costly. In order for justice to be served and satisfied, someone has to be punished for the offenses against God. Jesus knew in advance that He was going to pay the price for justice by suffering the penalty for all of the offenses of mankind. When He was hung on a cross and crucified, He not only took all of our sins upon Himself, He also took all the punishment for our sins. All of the Curse of the Law was unleashed upon Him, and He became a curse by hanging on a tree until He was dead.

> *Isaiah 53:4-5, 8 - Surely He took up our pain and bore our suffering, yet* ***we considered Him punished by God, stricken by Him, and afflicted****. But He was pierced for our transgressions, He was crushed for our iniquities; the* ***punishment that brought us peace was on Him****, and by His wounds we are healed. ... By* ***oppression and judgment He was taken away****. Yet who of His generation protested? For He was* ***cut off from the land of the living****; for the transgression of my people* ***He was punished****.*

> *Galatians 3:13 -* ***Christ redeemed us from the curse of the law by becoming a curse for us****, for it is written: "Cursed is everyone who is hung on a pole." (quoting Deuteronomy 21:23)*

Additionally, the Law states that any person's sins can be remembered by God for punishment to the third and fourth generation of their descendants, and some curses even go as far as the tenth generation. (see Exodus 20:5; Deuteronomy 23:22-23) When this happens, the person who sinned or one of their descendants suffers the punishment on account of their ancestors as if they are guilty of their ancestors' sins. But now, because all of our sins back to our original ancestor Adam were remembered by God when they were put upon Jesus on the cross, God remembers our sins no more. This does not mean that God has caught a case of amnesia. It means that everything that we, and our ancestors, have ever done or will ever do that does not adhere to God's perfect standard was brought to account and has already been punished. And so, since our sins have already been remembered and punished, God will never punish us for them again.

> *Hebrews 8:12 - "For* ***I will forgive*** *their wickedness and will* ***remember their sins no more.****" (quoting Jeremiah 31:31-34)*

As a perfect administrator of justice, there is no double jeopardy in God's court. Therefore, because all of the penalty that we deserve was unleashed on Jesus, we can be confident that the sicknesses included in the curse of the Law, which includes every illness, has been satisfied in full on our behalf. Jesus took what we deserve so that we receive what we do not deserve. If we truly believe what Jesus has done for us, then we can live by faith as those who know that it is literally against the Law for sickness to touch us. It's simply unjust!

Sickness Caused by the Devil

When Adam and Eve allowed themselves to be deceived by the devil back in the Garden of Eden, they rejected God as their God and unknowingly transferred all of mankind to be the under authority of the evil one. Therefore, the devil is referred to in the Scriptures as the prince and ruler of this world, the god of this age, and the spirit at work in the sons of disobedience. (see John 12:31, 14:30; 2 Corinthians 4:4; Ephesians 2:2) When God is our God, we have freedom, life, and authority over all creation but under satan's rule, we are subjected to deception, oppression, and the constant fear of death.

> *1 John 3:8a - The* ***one who does what is sinful is of the devil,*** *because the devil has been sinning from the beginning.*

> *1 John 5:19b - ...the* ***whole world is under the control of the evil one.***

The devil and his agents have been plaguing people since the beginning with all sorts of torments, compulsions, addictions, illnesses, and infirmities. In fact, there are many different types of ungodly spirits specifically listed throughout the Old and New Testaments including but not limited to spirits of jealousy, obstinance, evil, sorrow, lying, enticing, anguish, vanity, vexation, judgment, burning, Egypt, familiarity, perversity, judgment, deep sleep, stupor, error, heaviness, fainting, darkness, grief, scattering, enemy, whoredom, falsehood, uncleanness, and infirmity. These are in addition to the demonic spirits that Jesus cast out of sick people to heal them of diseases, which are listed out specifically in the next chapter, and the spirits that will be unleashed in the last days to gather the kings of the world to the battle of Armageddon. Even this list does not begin to cover all the varieties of evil spirits that are at work for the devil to carry out his many wicked schemes against mankind.

These messengers of the evil one are called demons or little devils. Demons are supernatural spirits of an evil nature which compel or entice people to erroneous beliefs or actions, torment them to mental or physical instability, or oppress them in various ways with intent to incapacitate and destroy. Their primary objective, however, is to avert people away from knowing, worshiping, and serving the One True God.

In fact, it was commonly believed among the Jews that demons were the spirits of the false gods of other nations of this world. Therefore, anyone who was oppressed by an evil spirit was suspected of worshipping false gods and, if this was the case then, it was generally presumed they deserved their torment. This belief makes sense in light of the fact that, in the days when the whole world was under the deceptive influence of the evil one, God had called upon their ancestor Abraham to enter into covenant with Him. God promised to be God to him. Therefore, the Jews were the only people on earth who had the One True God, the Most High God, the Almighty God as their God. This promise to be their God included His divine protection from the evil one even though the rest of the world would still be subject to his oppression. (see Genesis 17:7-8; Exodus 6:7) When God gave the Law to His people, this promise to be their defender against all enemies became a blessing for the righteous who obeyed His perfect standard. (see Exodus 23:22) Accordingly, it was common for any Jew oppressed by devils to be shunned as a blasphemer and Jews commonly regarded it as normal for a Gentile (non-Jew) to be mildly to severely oppressed by demons due to their lack of covenant with the God of Israel.

During His ministry, Jesus revealed the connection between demonic oppression and sickness in both Jews and Gentiles alike. In several instances, without a hint of fear, suspicion, or condemnation, Jesus healed people by commanding devils out of them. One woman had been crippled by a spirit of infirmity for eighteen years and Jesus exercised His authority as the Son of the Most High God to set the woman free from the evil spirit's oppression. He directly attributed her infirmity to the work of the devil.

> *Luke 13:16 - "Then should not this woman, a daughter of Abraham,* ***whom Satan has kept bound for eighteen long years,*** *be set free on the Sabbath day from what bound her?"*

Regardless of the fact that people were being healed from infirmities and afflictions caused by demons, the religious leaders constantly questioned Jesus' authority and consistently accused Him of working for the devil. In response, Jesus told them how He was going to overpower the devil once and for all—binding him and his influence in the earth.

> *Mark 3:26-27 NASB - "If Satan has risen up against himself and is divided, he cannot stand, but he is finished! "But no one can enter the strong man's house and plunder his property unless he* ***first binds the strong man****, and then he will plunder his house."*

You see, in order for Jesus to have authority over the ruler of this world, He would have to be God—and He was. However, Jesus had willingly subjected Himself to the limitations of mankind by being born in a flesh like ours. This made him just as vulnerable as any other human being to the schemes of the evil one and his reign of death.

Therefore, the first thing that the devil tried to do was to kill Jesus at birth by instigating the murder of every male born in Jesus' birthplace of Bethlehem. But God protected His Son by sending an angel to warn His earthly parents of the danger. (see Matthew 2) Later, when Jesus was about thirty years old, Jesus went into the wilderness to be tested and tried by the devil for forty days. (see Mark 1:11-13) In the wilderness, satan challenged Jesus with every temptation, including worshiping him instead of God. Also, the evil one most likely commanded leagues of demons to harass, irritate, and entice Jesus to give way to evil desires or actions. (see Luke 4:1-13) However, because the Holy Spirit gave Jesus the indwelling nature of God, He had God-given strength to resist every temptation that satan schemed. In fact, throughout the entirety of Jesus' life, He never sinned, not even in His heart. (see Hebrews 4:15)

Therefore, God remained Jesus' God. By not caving into sin, Jesus never gave the devil any authority over Him. This is the opposite of what Adam and Eve had done when they were enticed to sin in Eden which allowed the evil one to rule over them. This meant that Jesus rightfully retained God-given freedom, life, and authority over all creation the way God had originally intended for man, and He was also entitled to divine protection and everlasting life afforded to the righteous. Jesus could have even allowed God to transfer Him up to eternal life and blessings without experiencing death as God had previously done for Enoch and Elijah. (see Genesis 5:24; 2 Kings 2:11)

Instead, Jesus willingly allowed the evil one to reign over Him, even unto death. When the time came for Jesus to offer Himself up to the powers of darkness, He knew the time had come to bind the strong man and render him powerless. The devil entered into Judas and caused him to betray Jesus to those who sought to kill Him. As the night progressed, Jesus did not protest the events that led to His death, and He never enlisted supernatural support or defense. He willingly subjected Himself to the evil one's plan.

> *John 13:2, 27 - The evening meal was in progress, and* ***the devil had already prompted Judas****, the son of Simon Iscariot, to betray Jesus. ... As soon as Judas took the bread,* ***Satan entered into him****. So Jesus told him, "What you are about to do, do quickly."*

> *Luke 22:52-53 - Then Jesus said to the chief priests, the officers of the temple guard, and the elders, who had come for him, "Am I leading a rebellion, that you have come with swords and clubs? Every day I was with you in the temple courts, and you did not lay a hand on me.* ***But this is your hour--when darkness reigns****."*

In fact, one of the first times that Jesus ever spoke of the death He was going to die was when He referred to the story of Moses with the Israelites in the wilderness. (see John 3:14) In the historical account, the Israelites had complained against God and His appointed servant, Moses.

Therefore, poisonous serpents had been released against them to bite them and kill them. God instructed Moses to make an exact replica of the biting serpents out of bronze, place it upon a pole, and lift it up high for everyone to see. Anyone who looked at the snake on the pole was healed and lived. (see Numbers 21:4-9)

When Jesus was on the cross, the powers of darkness were allowed to reign over Him including wicked men and armies of demons. (see Psalm 22:11-18) In addition to this, the souls of every descendant of Adam (also known as sons of disobedience) were drawn upon Jesus on the cross. (see John 12:32) Jesus became an enemy of God and an exact replica of the nature of rebellion and sin, which is the nature of the devil, the ancient serpent. This replica of the serpent was lifted up on a pole when Jesus was lifted up on the cross. When Jesus died, it appeared that the evil one had triumphed forever over mankind and the powers of darkness had extinguished the Light of God. But on the third day, the Most High God raised Jesus from the dead, delivering Him forever from the devil's reign of death. (see Romans 6:9-10) Jesus was born again to everlasting life in a resurrection body that will never decline or decay. By entering into death and darkness, Jesus did not escape them—He overcame and conquered them. Through this, He invalidated and demolished the power and authority of the evil one over us forever. The strong man, satan, has been bound by One stronger than him.

> *Hebrews 2:14-15 - Since the children have flesh and blood, He too shared in their humanity so that* ***by His death He might break the power of him who holds the power of death--that is, the devil--*** *and free those who all their lives were held in slavery by their fear of death.*

> *1 John 3:8b - The reason the Son of God appeared was to* ***destroy the devil's work****.*

This means that just like the Israelites were healed by looking at the snake on the pole, everyone who looks to Jesus' sacrifice on the cross, believing that He is Lord and that God raised Him from the dead, receives eternal life and the blessings of the righteous. We have been freed from the rule of the devil and can live by faith as those who have already triumphed over death. Moreover, because the evil one no longer has mastery over us, his messengers, evil spirits, and little devils have absolutely no right to afflict us in any way. Any mental or physical illness, disease, or infirmity that the devil or his demons try to put on us can be rebuked, cast out, expelled, and rejected as we place our faith in Jesus.

Forgiven, Cancelled, Disarmed

In this chapter, we have witnessed the destruction of our enemies through our faith in the death and resurrection of Jesus just like the Israelites walked through the waters of the Red Sea and saw the destruction of their enemies. As a quick review, Jesus became sin for us, taking all of our sins upon Himself so that we can have a perfect record of obedience before God—we are forgiven. Jesus became a curse for us, taking all of our punishment upon Himself so that we never have to suffer penalty for our sins and errors again—the charges against us have been cancelled. Jesus became God's enemy for us so that we can be free from the devil's rule and the fear of death—the evil one has been disarmed.

> *Colossians 2:13-15 - When you were dead in your sins and in the uncircumcision of your flesh, God made you alive with Christ. He* ***forgave us all our sins****, having* ***canceled the charge of our legal indebtedness, which stood against us and condemned us****; He has taken it away, nailing it to the cross. And having* ***disarmed the powers and authorities****, He made a public spectacle of them,* ***triumphing over them by the cross****.*

In the original Passover, the Israelites were delivered from Pharaoh's dominion and transferred from the land of slavery into safety in the wilderness. In our eternal Passover, through the resurrection of Jesus, we have been delivered from the power of the evil one and transferred from the kingdom of darkness into the Kingdom of Light where there is freedom, blessing, and perpetual health.

> *Colossians 1:13-14 ESV - He has* ***delivered us from the domain of darkness*** *and* ***transferred us to the kingdom of His beloved Son****, in whom we have redemption, the forgiveness of sins.*

Jesus overcame every cause every cause of sickness and infirmity so that health and healing are ours to receive as a free gift through faith.

Chapter Three
YESHUA

After the Israelites walked through the rolled-away waters of the Red Sea and saw God stretch out His hand to destroy their enemies, they worshipped by singing the Song of Moses. This is how the song begins:

> *Exodus 15:2 ESV - The LORD is my strength and my song, and He* ***has become my salvation****; this is my God, and I will praise Him, my father's God, and I will exalt Him.*

In this song, the Hebrew word the Israelites used to describe God as their *salvation* is *yeshua,* which in its simplest form means *God saves*. However, if we dig a little deeper into the meaning of yeshua and how it is used in the Scriptures, it includes *God's help, deliverance, healing, prosperity, and victory over enemies*. Through the course of the Passover, God did all of these things for His people in one event. They stood on the banks of the Red Sea, saved from harsh slavery because God helped them and delivered them from their oppressors. At the same time, God healed them of all of their diseases and prospered them by causing the Egyptians to give them great treasures. (see Psalm 105:37; Exodus 12:36) Ultimately, God gave them total victory over their enemies by burying the world's most powerful man and the strength of his army in the sea. They saw all of this with their own eyes, experienced it in their own bodies, and walked to freedom on their own feet. Imagine how they sang this song and worshiped God with all of their hearts!

As great and marvelous as this deliverance was, we know that this Old Testament event is merely a prophetic shadow of the greater work of salvation God provided by sending His Messiah. Accordingly, when the angel spoke to Mary and Joseph to instruct them to name their son Jesus, he spoke to them in Hebrew and told them to name Him Yeshua.

> *Matthew 1:21 - She will give birth to a son, and* ***you are to give Him the name Jesus, because He will save His people from***

their sins. *" (see also Luke 1:31)*

In Jewish culture, and therefore in the Scriptures, a person's name is highly significant in describing their character and/or God's purpose for their life. Oftentimes, God instructed expectant parents about the name they were to give their child because of the plans He created for the unborn child before the foundation of the earth. In view of this, it is through *Jesus* our *Yeshua* that we receive salvation, deliverance, healing, and sustenance that far surpasses the original Passover experience of the Israelites.

God's Will Revealed

As Jesus/Yeshua grew to manhood and began His ministry, He clearly expressed God's purpose of salvation through His life. He did not come to condemn, to judge, or to oppress but to forgive, show mercy, and set free.

> *John 3:17 - For God did not send His Son into the world to condemn the world, but* ***to save the world through Him.***
>
> *John 12:47 - "If anyone hears my words but does not keep them, I do not judge that person. For I did not come to judge the world, but* ***to save the world.*** *"*

This said, the salvation/yeshua Jesus offers is not limited to His death on a cross to pay for our sin so that we can go to heaven when we die. Eternal life and a heavenly home is part of what He came to give us, but we should not stop there because He did not stop there. Jesus did not come only to die for us but also to live for us in order to reveal the perfect will of God in action. Jesus is the exact image of God in the earth and whatever Jesus did was exactly what God desired to be done in each situation. (see Hebrews 1:3; John 14:9) In fact, the very first time Jesus publicly presented Himself as a servant of God, He spoke nothing of His sacrificial death but only of the things He would do to fulfill God's purpose while He lived.

> *Luke 4:18-19 - "The Spirit of the Lord is on me, because He has anointed me to* ***proclaim good news to the poor****. He has sent me to* ***proclaim freedom for the prisoners*** *and* ***recovery of sight for***

> ***the blind**, to **set the oppressed free**, to **proclaim the year of the Lord's favor**." (quoting Isaiah 61:1-2)*

After making this declaration of His identity and mission, Jesus set out to do it. He healed the sick, cleansed lepers, opened the eyes of the blind and the ears of the deaf, cast demons out of people, and raised the dead. When we read the Gospel accounts about the things Jesus did while He was on earth, we see that He did not just speak about salvation, eternal life, and the Kingdom of God—He manifested it by demonstrating instant salvation, deliverance, healing, sustenance, and the life-giving power of God. This is what Yeshua looks like! This is the salvation of our God come to life! Here is a chart of some of Jesus' healings, signs, and wonders.

The Blind Receive Sight	
2 Blind Men	Matthew 9
Blind Man	Mark 8
Man Born Blind	John 9
Blind Man	Matthew 20, Mark 10, Luke 18
The Deaf Hear	
Deaf and Mute Man	Mark 7
Deaf and Mute Boy	Mark 9
The Lame Walk	
Man Lame 38 years	John 5
Paralyzed Man	Matthew 9, Mark 2, Luke 5
The Sick Are Healed	
Woman Bleeding 12 Years	Matthew 9, Mark 5, Luke 8
Woman with Fever	Matthew 8, Mark 1, Luke 4
Man Near Death	Matthew 8, Luke 7
Boy Very Sick/Near Death	John 4
Man with Swelling/Dropsy	Luke 14
Deformed Hand Restored	Matthew 12, Mark 3, Luke 6
Cut Off Ear Restored	Luke 22
Lepers are Cleansed	
Leper	Matthew 8, Mark 1, Luke 5
Ten Lepers	Luke 17

The Dead are Raised	
Girl in Death Bed	Matthew 9, Mark 5, Luke 8
Man in Coffin at Funeral	Luke 7
Man in Grave Four Days	John 11
Demons are Cast Out	
Boy with Violent Seizures	Matthew 17, Mark 9, Luke 9
Girl with Tormenting Spirit	Matthew 15, Mark 7
Man with Evil/Unclean Spirit	Mark 1, Luke 4
Mute Man	Matthew 12, Luke 11
Woman Crippled 18 Years	Luke 13
Man Driven to Insanity	Matthew 8, Mark 5, Luke 8
Mute Man	Matthew 9

But Jesus was not limited to these miracles or to these illnesses. In fact, these examples are just the highlights that the writers of the Gospels chose to write about for our edification. However, these writers also made it definitively clear that Jesus healed ALL diseases for those who came to Him in faith.

> *Matthew 4:23-24 - Jesus went throughout Galilee, teaching in their synagogues, proclaiming the good news of the kingdom,* ***and healing every disease and sickness among the people****. News about Him spread all over Syria, and people brought to Him* ***all who were ill with various diseases, those suffering severe pain, the demon-possessed, those having seizures, and the paralyzed; and He healed them****.*

> *Matthew 9:35 - Jesus went through all the towns and villages, teaching in their synagogues, proclaiming the good news of the kingdom and* ***healing every disease and sickness****.*

> *Matthew 12:15 - Aware of this, Jesus withdrew from that place. A large crowd followed Him, and* ***He healed all who were ill****.*

> *Matthew 14:35-36 - And when the men of that place recognized Jesus, they sent word to all the surrounding country. People brought* ***all their sick*** *to Him and begged Him to let the sick just touch the edge of his cloak, and* ***all who touched it were healed****.*

Matthew 15:30-31 - Great crowds came to Him, bringing ***the lame, the blind, the crippled, the mute and many others, and laid them at His feet; and He healed them****. The people were amazed when they saw the mute speaking, the crippled made well, the lame walking and the blind seeing. And they praised the God of Israel.*

Mark 1:32-34, 39 - That evening after sunset the people brought to ***Jesus all the sick and demon-possessed****. The whole town gathered at the door, and* ***Jesus healed many who had various diseases. He also drove out many demons****, but He would not let the demons speak because they knew who He was. ... So He traveled throughout Galilee, preaching in their synagogues and* ***driving out demons****.*

Mark 3:10-11 - For He had ***healed many****, so that those with diseases were pushing forward to touch Him. Whenever the* ***impure spirits saw Him, they fell down before Him*** *and cried out, "You are the Son of God."*

Mark 6:54-56 - As soon as they got out of the boat, people recognized Jesus. They ran throughout that whole region and carried the sick on mats to wherever they heard He was. And wherever He went--into villages, towns or countryside--they placed the sick in the marketplaces. They begged Him to let them touch even the edge of his cloak, and ***all who touched it were healed****.*

Luke 4:40-41 - At sunset, the people brought to Jesus ***all who had various kinds of sickness, and laying His hands on each one, He healed them****. Moreover,* ***demons came out of many people,*** *shouting, "You are the Son of God!" But He rebuked them and would not allow them to speak, because they knew He was the Messiah.*

Luke 6:17-19 - He went down with them and stood on a level place. A large crowd of his disciples was there and a great number of people from all over Judea, from Jerusalem, and from the coastal region around Tyre and Sidon, who had come to hear

> *Him and to be healed of their diseases.* ***Those troubled by impure spirits were cured, and the people all tried to touch Him, because power was coming from Him and healing them all.***
>
> *Luke 7:21 - At that very time Jesus* ***cured many who had diseases, sicknesses and evil spirits, and gave sight to many who were blind.***
>
> *Luke 9:11 - ...But the crowds learned about it and followed Him. He welcomed them and spoke to them about the kingdom of God, and* ***healed those who needed healing****.*
>
> *John 6:2 - ...And a great crowd of people followed Him because they saw* ***the signs He had performed by healing the sick****.*
>
> *John 20:30 - Jesus performed* ***many other signs*** *in the presence of His disciples, which are not recorded in this book.*
>
> *John 21:25 - Jesus did* ***many other things as well****. If every one of them were written down, I suppose that even the whole world would not have room for the books that would be written.*

These healings and other miracles Jesus performed served as a sign to confirm Him as God's Son and the Messiah promised to Israel who is the Savior promised for all mankind. (see Matthew 12:15-21, quoting Isaiah 42:1-7, 35:5-6) These miracles also clearly reveal that it is God's will for the sick to be healed. As a matter of fact, it was never God's will for anybody to be sick in the first place.

Through Faith

But if it is so clearly God's will for the sick to be healed, then why isn't everyone healed? Why doesn't God just supernaturally intervene with divine authority to heal everyone one earth? Well, remember, all of mankind still has a dreadful sin problem because our ancestor Adam sold our entire species to the devil back in the Garden of Eden. When Adam disobeyed, death began to reign over us instead of life and sickness in our bodies is an indication of the reign of death. Without the God-appointed Savior God promised to Adam back in the beginning, we are all hopelessly doomed to die and remain vulnerable to every kind of sickness and disease. The only way for us to be reconnected to God, who is the source of life, is through the Savior who would crush the head of the serpent and terminate the evil one's rule over us. And the only way for us to receive the benefits this Savior offers us is through faith. This is significant because Jesus did not walk around healing every random stranger just because they were ill and He was a nice guy. Jesus did not heal everyone. He healed everyone who came to Him in faith.

In most cases, Jesus healed those who came to Him in faith because they believed Him to be the Messiah of God and, therefore, desperately sought Him out at any expense. In several incidents, Jesus healed people who cried out to Him as the Son of David as this was an open declaration of their faith that Jesus is the descendant of David who fulfills God's promises of a Savior. (see Matthew 9:27, 15:22; Luke 18:38) In fact, there are only a few examples of Jesus healing someone without being pursued as their Healer or Savior. Even so, in one case it was because they were dead and in most of the other instances of this, it was a demonstrative teaching for His disciples or as a rebuke to religious bystanders. (see Matthew 8:14-15, 12:9; Luke 7:13-15, 14:1-6; John 5:6-9, 9:1) Additionally, Jesus never healed a religious person who came to test Him or demand healing as a sign to prove Himself. In these cases, Jesus merely pointed to the plentiful miracles and healings He had performed for other people as irrefutable proof of His God-given authority. (see John 10:37-38, 14:10; Matthew 12:39)

By His Wounds

But God-given authority is not enough. In order to work miracles of salvation, deliverance, healing, and sustenance, a price had to be paid. Think of it this way: If you have signing privileges on a bank account, then you have authority to write checks. But if there is no money in the bank account, then your authority is useless. Jesus knew in advance that He was going to the cross to pay the price for us to be saved, which included taking all of our sicknesses upon Himself. Therefore, the healings that Jesus performed during His ministry on earth also served to confirm Him as the Suffering Servant of God who would be crushed and wounded so that we can be healed.

Matthew 8:16-17 - When evening came, many who were demon-possessed were brought to Him, and He drove out the spirits with a word and healed all the sick. ***This was to fulfill what was spoken through the prophet Isaiah: "He took up our infirmities and bore our diseases."*** *(quoting Isaiah 53:4-5)*

As we covered in the last chapter, all of our sins and all of the punishment we deserve was laid upon Jesus until the curse of the Law, which includes every form of sickness, was satisfied. In addition to this, Jesus was beaten, whipped, pricked, and stabbed until finally His hands and feet were nailed to the cross where He hung until He was dead. Through this, our illnesses, infirmities, and all forms of brokenness were laid upon Him until He was destroyed. In order for us to receive healing from all maladies and disorders, Jesus had to pay the price for them by taking them upon Himself as part of His suffering on our behalf.

Isaiah 53:4-5 - Surely He ***took up our pain and bore our suffering****, yet we considered Him punished by God, stricken by Him, and afflicted. But He was* ***pierced*** *for our transgressions, He was* ***crushed*** *for our iniquities; the punishment that brought us peace was on Him, and* ***by His wounds we are healed****.*

Most English translations of the Hebrew in this passage do not adequately express what Jesus did for us when He took our sicknesses upon Himself. When Matthew quoted this Scripture in his Gospel account, his interpretation was far more accurate by saying *infirmities* and *diseases* rather than *pain* and *suffering*. For example, the word translated from Hebrew as *pain* includes pain but in most other passages where this word is used, it is translated as *sickness*. The definition of this word from Hebrew is *sickness, malady, pain, infirmity, disease* and includes *anxiety, grief, sadness, evil,* and *calamities*. Plus, it stems from a Hebrew root word that means *to be or become sick, weak, ill, diseased, afflicted, sore, wounded, or grieved*. Additionally, the Hebrew word for *suffering,* which Matthew translates as *diseases*, is defined as *physical pain, mental pain, anguish, pain of soul,* and *sorrow* and is from a root word for *feeling pain, making sore,* and *destruction unto death*. With an all-inclusive list like this, we can be assured that every malady, infirmity, and disease that may be plaguing us was put upon Jesus at the cross.

This prophetic Scripture from Isaiah goes on to say that believers would be healed by the wounds of the Suffering Servant and even articulates what some of those wounds would be. God's Chosen One would be pierced, crushed, and wounded so that God's people can be cured, made whole, and healed. Digging into these words can give us insight into the ways that God's Servant would suffer.

Suffering	Meaning/Definition
Pierced	to break, pierce through, perforate, lay open; to be slain; to have one's honor violated; to be wounded fatally
Crushed	to be broken or beaten into pieces; to be bruised or destroyed; to be humiliated or oppressed; to be smited or trampled
Wounds	bruises, stripes, blows, hurts, marks of strokes on the skin

When the time came for Jesus to suffer, He grieved in anguish until He sweat drops like blood in the Garden of Gethsemane. (see Luke 22:44) Then, He was betrayed by a close friend, arrested like a criminal, condemned by the religious leaders, and was handed over to the governing authorities. (see Mark 14:53-65, 15:1) The guards spit on Him, struck Him, and slapped Him in the face. (see John 18:22; Matthew 26:67) They flogged Him with rods and with Roman whips that had metal spikes at the ends which ripped into His flesh—a punishment so cruel and severe that Roman citizens were exempt from this type of torture. They cut into His skull with a crown of thorns, stripped Him of His clothes, mocked Him, and struck Him on the head with rods again and again. (see Matthew 27:26-31) After all of this, they made Him carry His own cross to the place of His execution where they hammered nails into His hands and feet and slammed the cross into the upright position in order to hang Him until He was destroyed. (see John 19:16-18) After He died, a soldier sliced through His side with a spear to confirm that He was fully and completely dead. (see John 19:34) Through these things, and in fulfillment of the Scriptures, Jesus was pierced, crushed, and wounded until He no longer resembled a human being.

Isaiah 52:14 - Just as there were many who were appalled at

> *Him-- **His appearance was so disfigured beyond that of any human being and His form marred beyond human likeness**.*

But on the third day, God raised Jesus from the dead before His body had seen any decay. (see Psalm 16:10) Jesus triumphed over every disease, infirmity, infection, oppression, and even death by the power of God! His resurrection is proof that His sacrifice was accepted by God as His perishable body was regenerated into an imperishable resurrection body full of life, strength, and vigor.

However, even on Jesus' resurrection body, there were some wounds that remained. Jesus even allowed His disciples to see and touch the nail piercings in His hands and the spear cut in His side as a demonstration that He truly had been raised from the dead. (see John 20:25-27) But these wounds confirm more than just His resurrection. These piercings confirm His covenant of healing for us.

As we have discussed a bit in prior chapters, covenants are sealed with blood as a guarantee of the covenantal terms. For example, when two people enter into a covenant with each other, it is called *cutting a covenant*. Typically, each person would cut themselves on the palms of their hands or their wrists until they bled and then shake hands or make contact on their wrists with one another in order to mix their blood. This was to symbolize that they had become one with one another, taking on one another's assets, responsibilities, privileges, weaknesses, allies, and enemies as if they were their own, even unto death. Then they would each allow the covenant wound to heal, leaving a visible scar on their palms or wrists. These scars served as a reminder to them of their covenant relationship and obligation to the other person even if they did not see their covenant partner for long periods of time. Biblically speaking, Jonathan and David cut covenant with one another in this way. (see 1 Samuel 18:3)

In line with this, the wounds on Jesus' hands remain permanently as visible evidence of His covenant with us. The scar in His side reveals that He took on our weaknesses, adversaries, and our greatest enemy of death at the cost of His own life. In exchange, we receive His assets, privileges, strength, wholeness, health, and resurrection life because we trust that we are in covenant with Him through faith.

1 Peter 2:23-24 - When they hurled their insults at Him, He did not retaliate; when He suffered, He made no threats. Instead, He entrusted Himself to Him who judges justly. "He himself bore our sins" in His body on the cross, so that we might die to sins and live for righteousness; ***"by His wounds you have been healed."***

Again, the way that we outwardly display that we are in a covenant relationship with Jesus is through baptism. By being baptized into the name of Jesus/Yeshua, we are submerged into the salvation, deliverance, healing, and sustenance that is available to us through faith in Him.

The Name of Jesus/Yeshua

Covenant agreements were also entered into by each partner giving the other their robe or cloak, their weapons, and their signet rings to symbolize their total identification with the other. Trading garments indicated complete access to the covenant partner's status, identity, and assets. Swapping weapons symbolized an absolute pledge of defense against any enemy, placing each partner's power and might at the other's disposal. Exchanging rings granted each partner full permission to command, direct, approve, and forbid anything under the authority of the other. By possessing these things, each partner could function in the name of the other as if they themselves were that person, even in their absence.

In light of this, we can see more clearly how Jesus entered into covenant with us. When Jesus was born as a man, He took on our garment of flesh as a descendant of Adam, He took on our enemies, and He limited Himself under the authorities in this world. In exchange for this, when we believe in Him and enter into covenant with Him by faith, we become born again as children of God, we are given free access to God's power to combat every enemy that rises against us, and we receive authority in the name of Jesus as His representatives in the earth to do everything that He is authorized by God to do.

Therefore, let us grasp the authority that we now have in the name of Jesus as His covenant partners. Jesus was God in the flesh but humbled Himself and allowed Himself to be disgraced, rejected, beaten, and executed at the hands of men so that God's eternal plan to redeem us would be fulfilled. In return for this level of submission and selfless obedience to God for the purposes of God's Kingdom, God raised Jesus up to the place of utmost authority over all creation, second only to God Himself. Therefore, the name of Jesus carries with it a God-given authority that is higher than any other name in the whole universe and demolishes even the power of death.

> *Philippians 2:9-11 - Therefore* ***God exalted Him to the highest place and gave Him the name that is above every name****, that at the name of Jesus every knee should bow, in heaven and on earth and under the earth, and every tongue acknowledge that Jesus Christ is Lord, to the glory of God the Father.*

> *Ephesians 1:20-21 - He raised Christ from the dead and seated Him at his right hand in the heavenly realms,* ***far above all rule and authority, power and dominion, and every name that is invoked****, not only in the present age but also in the one to come.*

This means that now, as His covenant partners and as children of God, we who believe that Jesus is Lord have the same status before God, the same power of God working with us and for us, and the same authority Jesus has. In the name of Jesus, we have power and authority over every infirmity and disease that may try to attack or plague us, and even over all creation.

> *John 14:12-14 - "Very truly I tell you, whoever believes in Me will do the works I have been doing, and they will do even greater things than these, because I am going to the Father. And* ***I will do whatever you ask in My name****, so that the Father may be glorified in the Son. You may* ***ask Me for anything in My name, and I will do it****."*

> *John 16:23-24 - "In that day you will no longer ask Me anything. Very truly I tell you,* ***My Father will give you whatever you ask in My name****. Until now you have not asked for anything in My name. Ask and you will receive, and your joy will be complete."*

As a matter of fact, in addition to demonstrating His authority through

His own ministry, Jesus shared His authority with His disciples while He was still with them to demonstrate to them beyond a doubt that it is His and God's will for the sick to be healed through faith in His name. Before His suffering, death, and resurrection, when the Lord had sent out His twelve disciples and later the seventy-two, He gave them authority over every disease, unclean spirits, and the power of the evil one.

> *Matthew 10:1, 7-8 - Jesus called His twelve disciples to Him and* ***gave them authority to drive out impure spirits and to heal every disease and sickness****. ... As you go, proclaim this message: 'The kingdom of heaven has come near.'* ***Heal the sick, raise the dead, cleanse those who have leprosy, drive out demons****. Freely you have received; freely give.*

> *Luke 10:17, 19 - The seventy-two returned with joy and said, "Lord, even the demons submit to us* ***in Your name****." ... I have given you* ***authority to trample on snakes and scorpions and to overcome all the power of the enemy; nothing will harm you****."*

Now after His resurrection, because His blood has been shed to pay the price in full for our sin and sickness and because His sacrifice has been accepted by God, Jesus sends His disciples out with ALL authority in heaven and on earth in His name to continue the work of bringing His Kingdom to earth as it is in heaven.

> *Matthew 28:18-20 - Then Jesus came to them and said, "****All authority in heaven and on earth has been given to Me****. Therefore go and make disciples of all nations,* ***baptizing them in the name of the Father and of the Son and of the Holy Spirit****, and teaching them to obey everything I have commanded you. And surely I am with you always, to the very end of the age."*

> *Mark 16:17-18 - "And these signs will accompany those who believe:* ***In My name*** *they will drive out demons; they will speak in new tongues; they will pick up snakes with their hands; and when they drink deadly poison, it will not hurt them at all; they will place their hands on sick people, and they will get well."*

When the first disciples set out to obey Jesus' command after His ascension to heaven, they continued to do the things Jesus had done during His ministry and what they had done when He previously shared His authority with them. Even though their covenant partner had gone far away for a while, with full rights in Jesus' name as His covenant partners, they healed the sick, raised the dead, cleansed the lepers, and cast out demons with the same approach, authority, and power of God that Jesus would use if He was there in person. (see the Book of Acts) All the while, they pointed to Jesus as the one and only Messiah and Savior sent by God and the One who was truly responsible for all of the miracles.

> *Acts 3:6-8, 16 - Then Peter said, "Silver or gold I do not have, but what I do have I give you.* ***In the name of Jesus Christ of Nazareth****, walk." Taking him by the right hand, he helped him up, and instantly the man's feet and ankles became strong. He jumped to his feet and began to walk. Then he went with them into the temple courts, walking and jumping, and praising God. ...* ***By faith in the name of Jesus****, this man whom you see and know was made strong.* ***It is Jesus' name*** *and the faith that comes through Him that has completely healed him, as you can all see."*

> *Acts 4:30 - "Stretch out your hand to heal and perform signs and wonders* ***through the name of your holy servant Jesus****."*

> *Acts 8:6-7, 12 - When the crowds heard Philip and saw the signs he performed, they all paid close attention to what he said. For with shrieks, impure spirits came out of many, and many who were paralyzed or lame were healed. ... But when they believed Philip as he proclaimed the good news of the kingdom of God and the* ***name of Jesus Christ****, they were baptized, both men and women.*

> *Acts 9:34 - "Aeneas," Peter said to him, "****Jesus Christ heals you****. Get up and roll up your mat." Immediately Aeneas got up.*

> *Acts 9:15 - But the Lord said to Ananias, "Go! This man [Paul] is my chosen instrument* ***to proclaim My name*** *to the Gentiles and their kings and to the people of Israel."*

Acts 10:43 - "All the prophets testify about Him [Jesus] that everyone who believes in Him receives forgiveness of sins ***through His name.****"*

Acts 16:18 - She kept this up for many days. Finally Paul became so annoyed that he turned around and said to the spirit, "In the name of Jesus Christ I command you to come out of her!" At that moment the [demonic] spirit left her.

Even though this is not a book about how to pray for the sick, when we understand Jesus' sacrifice and assignment for us, we can be assured that healing from all kinds of sicknesses and diseases is God's will for us. Jesus does not send His disciples out to give away something that we have not received for ourselves. The benefits of our salvation/yeshua through faith in Jesus are ours as His covenant partners and as children of God. The name of Jesus has not diminished in power since His resurrection, and His commission for us as His followers has not changed since the days of His first disciples.

Hebrews 13:8 - Jesus Christ is the same yesterday and today and forever.

This said, as powerful as the name of Jesus is, its authority is only available to those who believe Jesus is the Messiah sent by God. A group of men in Ephesus tried to use the name of Jesus to cast demons out of a man even though they were not followers of Jesus. As a result, the demon overpowered them and beat them up because, without covenant partnership, they had no right to use Jesus' name to do anything. (see Acts 19:13-16)

No Other Name

When Jesus cried out, "It is finished" on the cross, His work of salvation/yeshua for all mankind was complete. The price Jesus paid was completely sufficient to make provision for every single person in the world to be saved, healed, and delivered from evil. Moreover, it is unquestionably God's will and desire for all people to be saved.

1 Timothy 2:3-4 - This is good, and pleases God our Savior, ***who wants all people to be saved*** *and to come to a knowledge of the* *truth.*

2 Peter 3:9b - Instead He is patient with you, ***not wanting anyone to perish****, but everyone to come to repentance.*

However, not everyone receives salvation from God because not everyone will place their faith in Jesus as their Yeshua. Salvation is available only to those who are willing to give up all other gods, idols, and forms of spirituality to place our faith entirely in Jesus. There is only one God who created the Universe, and He has made no other arrangements, methods, or approaches for receiving His benefits.

Acts 4:12 - "Salvation is found in no one else, for there is ***no other name under heaven given to mankind by which we must be saved."***

It is also God's will for everyone to be healed but not everyone is healed. Sometimes, this means that we have to change our minds about our relationship with Jesus and how much we have actually allowed Him to be our Savior, the Lord of our life, and to show us His Yeshua. For all He has done for us, He is worthy of our undivided attention, allegiance, and trust. His name deserves to be first and highest in our lives and revered above all other names, methods, and remedies. So, with this in mind, let us press on to know Him and all He has done for us so that we can receive from Him everything He died to give us.

Chapter Four
SHABBAT SHALOM

When we do not understand God's love in light of what Jesus did for us, we can be led into erroneous beliefs. Sometimes, this means that we go questing after an emotional or physical experience of God's love rather than seeking the truth that makes us free. We may even doubt that we know God's love unless we "feel it." Other times, we redefine love to suit our own inclinations which usually involves making love blind to sin or denying that sin is sin. On the other hand, we might begin to fear that God does not really love us because we have done something wrong or that we have to do something in order to be worthy of God's love. But, God's love is not always a sensation, does not deny sin or say that sin is not sin, and is not based on our ability to live morally perfect lives. God's love says, "I love you so much that I gave my Son, Jesus, to shed His blood so that your sins are forgiven. Now there is nothing standing in the way of Me pouring out my grace and blessings to you. You can rest because we are at peace."

Even so, God's love can seem improbable when something happens in our lives which seems contrary to our concept of God being a loving Heavenly Father. This is particularly true when it comes to sickness. When we become sick, there is a tendency for fear to arise that we are being punished for something we have done. However, this would mean that we were still being judged by our own ability to meet God's standards rather than being recipients of His blessings, including healing, because of the finished work of Jesus. It was because of God's great love for us that Jesus took ALL of our punishment upon Himself. Therefore, we have nothing to fear and, even in the face of sickness or death, we do not need to doubt God's abounding goodwill toward us, including His will for us to be well.

> *1 John 4:18 - There is no fear in love. But* ***perfect love drives out fear, because fear has to do with punishment****. The one who*

fears is not made perfect in love.

The Hebrew word used to describe God's redemptive love for His people is *ahaba,* the same word used to describe the love of a bridegroom for his bride. It expresses passionate desire and delight, panting after something with willingness to do anything for it. For example, when God redeemed Israel out of slavery, they were the smallest and weakest nation on earth but God *ahaba*/loved His people so much that He rescued them and healed them with none feeble among them so that He could bless them as His own special people. (see Deuteronomy 7:8) Similarly, in the eternal Passover, Jesus *ahaba*/loves us so much that He offered His life to rescue us as His beloved Bride and was wounded for our healing, not because we have done anything to deserve it but because we have been chosen to be special to Him and cared for by Him in every way. (see Ephesians 5:28-32)

> *John 3:16-17 - For* ***God so loved the world that He gave His one and only Son,*** *that whoever believes in Him shall not perish but have eternal life. For God did not send His Son into the world to condemn the world, but to save the world through Him.*

> *1 John 3:16a -* ***This is how we know what love is****: Jesus Christ laid down His life for us.*

In everyday life, the word used to describe how this love is revealed is *chesed,* which is most often translated as *mercy*, and can also mean *lovingkindness* and *zealous goodwill.* As an example, Jesus was motivated by *chesed*/mercy in everything He did, particularly His healing miracles. Without condemnation, He forgave people's sins, cancelling the record of charges against them, which also freed them from their infirmities. Through His sacrifice, Jesus purchased for us never-ending *chesed*/mercies from God to cover us for all the errors we make on a daily basis. Two Old Testament people who particularly understood how the love of God is expressed through His mercy were Job and David. In essence, Job foresaw what Jesus came to do for us by including us in His death so that we can have a fresh start with God every day because our sins have already been punished and brought down to the pit. (see Job 14:13-17) Likewise, David understood what it means to receive from God what we do not deserve. He rejoiced with shouts of joy over the blessings, including healing, available to those whose sins are forgiven. (see Psalm 32)

All of this is to say that God loves us so much that He removed every obstacle that stood in the way of our ability to receive His blessings. Plus, He continually gives us a clean slate as if we had never sinned. Therefore, instead of chasing experiences of passion or hiding ourselves in doubt and shame, we can fearlessly rest with peace in our hearts and receive our healing as a free gift.

Rest for Our Souls

Through the course of the Passover, God healed the Israelites of their diseases and feebleness. Then, they walked into the wilderness and they came to an oasis which God miraculously changed from bitter to sweet. In this place, God promised the Israelites that, if they obeyed His voice, He would be their Physician and Healer, keeping them free from every disease and plague of Egypt.

> *Exodus 15:26 He [God] said, "If you listen carefully to the LORD your God and do what is right in His eyes, if you pay attention to His commands and keep all His decrees, I will not bring on you any of the diseases I brought on the Egyptians, for* ***I am the LORD, who heals you****."*

Soon after this, the Israelites grumbled out of hunger and expressed their desire to return to Egypt where they had eaten as much as they wanted. They seemed to have forgotten that the food they ate in Egypt was not free. They had been slaves, working under harsh task masters to build cities for an evil ruler. And so, the first instruction God gave them was put in place to forever remind them that He had redeemed them from slavery. This instruction was to keep the Sabbath. For six days they could gather what God provided for them. But on the seventh day, they were required to rest from all work and observe the Sabbath. (see Exodus 16)

The Hebrew word for *sabbath* means to *cease from exertion, to rest from labor*, and is used in other places to indicate *doing away with* something or *failure to produce*. Accordingly, to observe the Sabbath requires devoting the day to complete rest and doing no ordinary work. When God gave the Law to His people, the Sabbath became the fourth commandment. Anyone who desecrated the Sabbath or fails to observe the Sabbath must be cut off from the people of God or be put to death. (see Leviticus 23:3; Exodus 31:14-15)

This is significant because since the fall of Adam, all of mankind has been under the curse of sweat and toil with thorns and thistles. Everyone must work hard for their food and provision or die of starvation. Workaholism would seem to be the only correct approach to survival but instead, God gives His people rest. Rest is a gift from God to His people, to help them remember that He redeemed them from the bitterness of slavery and from the curse of sweat and toil. Observing the Sabbath is an act of trust in God's gracious provision and a way of identifying themselves as the people of the one true God, Creator of heaven and earth. Just like circumcision is the sign of inclusion in the covenant between God and Abraham, observing the Sabbath became a new sign that symbolizes inclusion in the redeemed people of God.

> *Exodus 16:29 NLT - "They [The people of Israel] must realize that* ***the Sabbath is the LORD's gift to you****. That is why He gives you a two-day supply on the sixth day, so there will be enough for two days. On the Sabbath day you must each stay in your place. Do not go out to pick up food on the seventh day."*

> *Deuteronomy 5:15 - "****Remember that you were slaves in Egypt*** *and that the LORD your God brought you out of there with a mighty hand and an outstretched arm. Therefore the LORD your God has commanded you to observe the Sabbath day."*

> *Exodus 31:13, 17 - "Say to the Israelites, 'You must observe my Sabbaths.* ***This will be a sign between Me and you*** *for the generations to come, so you may know that I am the LORD, who makes you holy. ...* ***It will be a sign between Me and the Israelites forever****, for in six days the LORD made the heavens and the earth, and on the seventh day He rested and was refreshed.' "*

In addition to every seventh day being a day of rest for the people of Israel, there are a number of other days throughout the year on which the Law prohibits ordinary work, particularly connected to the Feasts of

God. (see Leviticus 23) Instead of working overtime at specific times during the year that are important for securing a good harvest, the Law requires God's people to observe multiple days of mandatory rest. No ordinary work is permitted at all as they trust in God's faithfulness to abundantly supply all they need and take time to rejoice in all He has done. The most extreme example of this mandatory rest is on the Day of Atonement when all Israelites are required to do no ordinary work and humble themselves before God through fasting. Anyone who does any work or does not deny themselves on the Day of Atonement will be cut off from the people and destroyed by God.

> *Leviticus 23:28-32 - "**Do not do any work on that day**, because it is the Day of Atonement, when atonement is made for you before the LORD your God. **Those who do not deny themselves on that day must be cut off from their people. I will destroy from among their people anyone who does any work on that day. You shall do no work at all.** This is to be a lasting ordinance for the generations to come, wherever you live. **It is a day of sabbath rest for you, and you must deny yourselves.** From the evening of the ninth day of the month until the following evening you are to **observe your sabbath**."*

Needless to say, God takes rest very seriously. This is because rest is an outward display of covenant relationship with Him. Rest proves trust in Him. Rest demonstrates gratitude for His redemption.

In our eternal Passover, without Jesus, we are still subject to the Law of God, earning blessings or meriting curses through our own works. At the same time, we are slaves to sin because we cannot escape our own flesh and its desires and we are just as powerless as our ancestor Adam when it comes to obeying God. You could say that this means that we are all subject to a spiritual form of sweat and toil with thorns and thistles for our souls. But through Jesus' death and resurrection, we have been set free from the labor of the Law so that we can be at rest in His provision of righteousness and mercy. Jesus became our perfect sacrifice of atonement so that we can rest in our redemption as God's children. (see Romans 3:25) He said it this way:

> *Matthew 11:28-29 - "Come to me, all you who are weary and*

> *burdened, and **I will give you rest**. Take My yoke upon you and learn from Me, for I am gentle and humble in heart, and **you will find rest for your souls**."*

In other words, and as is reflected in Hebrew translations of the New Testament, Jesus is saying, "Come to me and I will give you Sabbath, a Sabbath for your soul." Jesus redeemed us from slavery to sin and from the curse of spiritual sweat and toil because our blessings no longer depend on our own obedience but His! This means that we can rest, cease from, and put away all of the things we are doing or not doing from a motive of earning God's blessings because we recognize that they will fail to produce anything of eternal value. Now, the only thing that has any value before God is our faith in Jesus.

To put it simply, our salvation, deliverance, healing, and sustenance is either based on what we do, or it is based on what Jesus did. When Jesus cried out on the cross, "It is finished," He either meant that it is finished or He meant that it is not quite done yet. Either the blood of Jesus works or it doesn't. Either He paid the price in full for our sins or He didn't. Either He took all of our punishment upon Himself or we can still be penalized. Either He conquered the devil or the devil still reigns over us. But if Jesus has done all of these things, which He has, then the only thing for us to do now is to be at rest in our hearts, immovably certain of God's faithfulness, power, ability, and willingness to bless us because of what Jesus has done for us.

Therefore, in order for us to honor and observe the eternal Sabbath that Jesus has given to us, we must cease from religious regulations, human commands, the ways and wisdom of this world, doing "good things," and anything else we might be trusting in somehow thinking we will earn or deserve God's favor or produce anything of value through them. We must also guard our freedom carefully from all forms of legalism, self-justification, and any teachings that imply that the blood of Jesus is not completely sufficient for our salvation, deliverance, healing, and sustenance.

> *Colossians 2:20-23* - ***Since you died with Christ to the elemental spiritual forces of this world, why, as though you still belonged to the world, do you submit to its rules**: "Do not*

handle! Do not taste! Do not touch!"? These rules, which have to do with things that are all destined to perish with use, are based on merely human commands and teachings. Such regulations indeed have an appearance of wisdom, with their self-imposed worship, their false humility and their harsh treatment of the body, but they lack any value in restraining sensual indulgence.

Colossians 2:16-17 - ***Therefore do not let anyone judge you by what you eat or drink, or with regard to a religious festival, a New Moon celebration or a Sabbath day****. These are a shadow of the things that were to come; the reality, however, is found in Christ.*

Galatians 4:8-9 - Formerly, ***when you did not know God, you were slaves to those who by nature are not gods****. But now that you know God--or rather are known by God--****how is it that you are turning back to those weak and miserable forces?*** *Do you wish to be enslaved by them all over again?*

Galatians 3:1-3 - You foolish Galatians! Who has bewitched you? Before your very eyes Jesus Christ was clearly portrayed as crucified. I would like to learn just one thing from you: ***Did you receive the Spirit by the works of the law, or by believing what you heard?*** *Are you so foolish? After beginning by means of the Spirit,* ***are you now trying to finish by means of the flesh?***

Romans 4:4-5 - Now to the one who works, wages are not credited as a gift but as an obligation. However, ***to the one who does not work but trusts God who justifies the ungodly, their faith is credited as righteousness****.*

Galatians 5:1 - ***It is for freedom that Christ has set us free****. Stand firm, then, and* ***do not let yourselves be burdened again*** *by a yoke of slavery.*

Rest is an indication of our understanding that God's mercy and blessings are truly undeserved and cannot be earned through any kind of work. If we are stressed because we are trying to deserve God's blessings through our own efforts, then our souls are not at rest. Every other religion in the world is full of restless people who never know where they stand with their god or higher power. But Jesus came so that we can be confident in our right standing with the Most High God because our faith is not in our own worthiness but in His and in His sacrifice that atoned for of our sins. Our rest in Him serves as a sign between Him and us that we trust in His redemption and that we are humble enough to admit that we have nothing of value to add to His atoning work.

We can also rest in faith that, because of Jesus' perfect obedience on our behalf, God is our Physician who heals us from all the diseases of this world. This said, sometimes, when we really need a blessing from God, which become particularly poignant when we are sick, it seems that we should exert ourselves more to "get right with God" through doing extra good things that we think God would want us to do. However, just like extra days of rest were required when working overtime seemed to be a more logical approach, it is the times when we need God most that He often calls us deeper into the rest that Jesus has provided for us.

Peace with God

The Hebrew word for *peace* is *shalom* and, in addition to peace from war, shalom includes *completeness, soundness, wholeness, safety, good health, prosperity, tranquility, contentment, friendship,* and *ease*. Shalom is a state of being where everything is working exactly as it should, and there is perfect harmony between all the many facets of life. Shalom in our bodies is when every organ, bone, joint, and ligament is functioning properly and according to God's design. Shalom with God is when we have right standing with Him because every hindrance to our relationship has been removed.

Since the fall of Adam, there has been an ongoing war between God and man. When there was no way for anyone to have peace with God, God made a way by sending His Son. As an example of God's approach to war and peace, when He sent the nation of Israel to war against enemy nations, He instructed them to first proclaim peace. (see Deuteronomy 20:10) Israel would extend an offer of peace to their enemies and, if this offer was accepted, the enemies would become servants of Israel. If the offer of peace was not accepted, the enemies would be destroyed. Shalom could only be attained through submission to the God of Israel.

In line with this, when God sent Jesus into the world which had become His enemy, Jesus came to proclaim peace. Jesus extended an offer of shalom with God to the Jews, who could not attain righteousness through their own efforts, and He extended the offer of shalom to Gentiles who previously had no hope of peace with the One True God.

> *Ephesians 2:17 - **He came and preached peace** to you who were far away and peace to those who were near.*

> *John 14:27 - "**Peace I leave with you; my peace I give you**. I do not give to you as the world gives. Do not let your hearts be troubled and do not be afraid."*

As is true in any war, terms of peace require a settling of accounts so that the parties can be reconciled. Whatever it was that caused the disruption that led to war must be brought to the surface and fully addressed or the peace agreement will prove to be inadequate and peace will not last. Through His perfect life and sacrificial death, Jesus singlehandedly settled the accounts for all of humanity to have peace with God by fulfilling God's legal requirements for a peace offering. (see Leviticus 3, 7)

> *Isaiah 53:5 - But He was pierced for our transgressions, He was crushed for our iniquities; **the punishment that brought us peace was on Him**, and by His wounds we are healed.*

> *Colossians 1:19-20 - For God was pleased to have all His fullness dwell in Him, and through Him to reconcile to Himself all things, whether things on earth or things in heaven, **by making peace through His blood, shed on the cross**.*

> *Romans 5:1 - Therefore, since we have been justified through faith, **we have peace with God through our Lord Jesus Christ**.*

The way we accept the terms of peace that Jesus offers is to love Him and obey Him as our Lord. (see John 14:15, 21, 23; 1 John 5:3-4) In the end, on the Day of Judgment, anyone who does not accept Jesus' terms of peace will be destroyed. This said, when we accept the offer of peace with God that Jesus extends to us, we no longer need to be anxious about anything or be concerned that God is treating us like an enemy, no matter what may be happening in our circumstances.

Philippians 4:6-7 - ***Do not be anxious about anything****, but in every situation, by prayer and petition, with thanksgiving, present your requests to God.* ***And the peace of God****, which transcends all understanding,* ***will guard your hearts and your minds in Christ Jesus****.*

Colossians 3:15 - ***Let the peace of Christ rule in your hearts****, since as members of one body you were called to peace. And be thankful.*

We have already referenced Isaiah 53 quite a bit in this book because it details the atoning work of Jesus for us and points us to our healing. But, as you probably know, Isaiah 53 comes right before Isaiah 54. Though we won't go into too much detail, I encourage you to read it for yourself because Isaiah 54 outlines some aspects that are significant for understanding the peace we have with God because Jesus fulfilled Isaiah 53. Through the sacrifice of the Suffering Servant of Isaiah 53, God established us in righteousness. This means that we are settled in right standing with Him, have peace with Him, and are secure in His care. (see v. 14) This also means that any enemy that attempts to attack us is not from God, including any natural or spiritual weapon forged against us and every tongue of accusation that contradicts the work of Christ on our behalf. (see v. 15-17) Therefore, we have assurance that no accusation against us is from God's mouth and that anything evil in our lives, including sickness, was not sent by Him. We no longer have to be concerned that anything has somehow disrupted the peace with God that Jesus secured for us and this means that we can have absolute confidence in our hearts and total security in our daily lives. Jesus paid the price for us to have perfect peace with God and the price included all that is required for us to be healed.

Shabbat Shalom

Psalm 92 is traditionally known as the psalm or song of the Sabbath. I encourage you to read Psalm 92 and see for yourself how clearly it expresses rejoicing over God's defeat of every enemy and the blessings He gives to His people. In addition to this, modern Jews have another song that is sung on the Sabbath. It is fun to sing, and nobody needs a lyric sheet because there are only two words in the whole song—*Shabbat shalom*. *Shabbat shalom* means *rest of peace*, and saying it to someone is a way of blessing them as if you were saying, "Have a peaceful day of rest," or, "May the Sabbath bring you peace."

I am not suggesting that we start obeying the Law or observing traditions but that we recognize that because of God's abounding love for us, Jesus came to bless us with eternal *shabbat shalom*, an everlasting rest of peace. Particularly when unfavorable circumstances or sickness cause us to doubt God's love for us, even if we have come to salvation and have seen God work miracles for us, we can be just like the grumbling Israelites, thinking we would be better off trusting in our own methods rather than resting in Him. This said, when our walk of faith becomes most challenging, the only thing we are told to strive to do is to enter into the rest and peace that has been provided for us through the work of Jesus.

> *Hebrews 4:9-11 ESV - So then, there remains* ***a Sabbath rest for the people of God****, for whoever has entered God's rest has also rested from his works as God did from His. Let us therefore* ***strive to enter that rest****, so that no one may fall by the same sort of disobedience.*

We can receive our healing from God if we will trust Jesus enough to enter into the everlasting shabbat shalom that He gives us as free gift and as a sign between Him and us that we are the children of God.

Chapter Five

YOUR FAITH HAS HEALED YOU

After the Passover, the Israelites lived in divine health in the wilderness for forty years. God sustained them in perfect health on a diet of manna from heaven and miracle water. God also prevented disease from striking those who acknowledged His right to their entire life by paying the ransom prescribed in the Law, which was used in serving the Tabernacle of God. (see Exodus 30:11-16) The only exceptions to this were incidents of their own disobedience that warranted plagues, sickness, and sometimes, sudden death. Plus, an entire generation of those who did not believe God was able to deliver on His promises died in the wilderness without inheriting what should have been rightfully theirs. (see Numbers 14:30)

Similarly, because Jesus is our eternal Passover Lamb and our Yeshua, healing and health is our birthright as born again believers and as God's children. Jesus is worthy of us offering our bodies to Him for the service of His Kingdom and of our trust that He knows how to maintain us in divine health. In fact, we should be the healthiest people on earth! In the event that we do become ill, we can be confident that sickness is not God's will for us and that we can receive our healing as a free gift of God's grace because of Jesus' sacrifice.

This said, it is no longer sin, the curse of the Law, or the devil that keeps us sick but our own unbelief in what Jesus did for us.

Healed by Faith

Approximately half of Jesus' healing miracles in the Scriptures are linked to the faith of someone involved. This is in addition to the countless healing miracles that many others received because they pursued Jesus out of faith even though their faith is not explicitly credited.

*Matthew 8:13 - Then Jesus said to the centurion, "Go! **Let it be*** *__done just as you believed__ it would." And his servant was healed at that moment.*

Matthew 9:29 - Then He touched their eyes and said, "__According to your faith__ let it be done to you."

Matthew 15:28 - Then Jesus said to her, "Woman, __you have great faith__! Your request is granted." And her daughter was healed at that moment.

Mark 2:5 - When __Jesus saw their faith__, He said to the paralyzed man, "Son, your sins are forgiven."

Luke 8:48 - Then He said to her, "Daughter, __your faith has healed you__. Go in peace."

Luke 17:19 - Then He said to him, "Rise and go; __your faith has made you well.__"

Luke 18:42 - Jesus said to him, "Receive your sight; __your faith has healed you.__"

Jesus did not judge or condemn anyone in any way for their sin before healing them, and He did not require confession of sin, proof of repentance, or any other preconditions for meriting healing. Though He occasionally tested the genuineness of the prospective recipient's faith and desire to be well, He was always able and willing to heal the sick that came to Him in faith.

Matthew 9:28 - When He had gone indoors, the blind men came to Him, and He asked them, __"Do you believe that I am able to do this?"__ "Yes, Lord," they replied.

John 5:6 - When Jesus saw him lying there and learned that he had been in this condition for a long time, He asked him, __"Do you want to get well?"__

Luke 5:12-13 NLT - In one of the villages, Jesus met a man with an advanced case of leprosy. When the man saw Jesus, he bowed with his face to the ground, begging to be healed. "Lord," he said, __"if You are willing, You can heal me__ and make me clean." Jesus reached out and touched him. __"I am willing," He said. "Be healed!"__ And instantly the leprosy disappeared.

Mark 9:21-24 NLT - "How long has this been happening?" Jesus asked the boy's father. He replied, "Since he was a little boy. The spirit often throws him into the fire or into water, trying to kill him. Have mercy on us and help us, if you can." ***"What do you mean, 'If I can'?" Jesus asked. "Anything is possible if a person believes."*** *The father instantly cried out, "I do believe, but help me overcome my unbelief!"*

In contrast, those who thought they could earn blessings from God based on their own righteousness received nothing from Jesus. For example, when the religious people in Jesus' day became upset and offended because of the people Jesus chose to heal, bless, and spend time with, He rebuked them for being blinded by their own pride and religion.

Matthew 9:12-13 NLT - When Jesus heard this, He said, ***"Healthy people don't need a doctor--sick people do."*** *Then He added, "Now go and learn the meaning of this Scripture:* ***'I want you to show mercy***, *not offer sacrifices.' For* ***I have come to call not those who think they are righteous, but those who know they are sinners."***

*John 9:39 NLT - Then Jesus told him, "I entered this world to render judgment--****to give sight to the blind and to show those who think they see that they are blind."***

In spite of all of their religious piety and good works, Jesus worked no miracles for them.

No Knowledge of Good and Evil

In the historical account of Israel, a little over a year after the Israelites had miraculously departed from Egypt, it was time for them to inherit the Promised Land. Moses sent spies into the land who returned with a report of the amazing abundance that the land produced. However, the inhabitants of the land were giants so large that the Israelites looked like grasshoppers by comparison. Therefore, ten out of the twelve spies did not believe that God was able to conquer their enemies and give them the land He had promised. The community of Israel believed the ten spies and murmured in protest against God, even though they had seen God deliver them from Egypt and the world's most powerful army. Therefore,

God informed them that the entire generation that did not believe would be unable to inherit the Promised Land. Only those under twenty years old who had no knowledge of good and evil would be able to inherit it. When the Israelites heard this, they decided it was possible for them to take the land after all, so they presumptuously charged into the Promised Land in their own strength even though God was not with them. They were defeated and humiliated by their enemies and, eventually, everyone from the unbelieving generation died in the wilderness without receiving what God had promised them. (see Numbers 13-14; Deuteronomy 1:19-46)

In our eternal Passover, through Jesus' life, death, and resurrection, He fulfilled the Law of Moses and made it obsolete as a means of obtaining righteousness. (see Hebrews 8:13) Consequently, we are no longer judged, blessed, or cursed according to the standard of the Old Covenant but according to the terms of the New Covenant, which is by faith. (see Hebrews 7:12; Romans 8:1-2) Sin has been done away with, and it is no longer sin that causes us to fall out of God's good graces. (see Hebrews 9:26) Rather, anyone who seeks to be righteous on their own merits instead of Jesus' righteousness falls from grace by plummeting from Jesus' perfection back to the hopeless depravity of our ancestor Adam. Anyone desiring to be justified and receive blessing from God through any form of legalism (which is the knowledge of good and evil) is required to keep the whole Law perfectly, something which no one in history except Jesus has ever been able to do.

> *Galatians 5:3-4 - Again I declare to every man who lets himself be circumcised that he is obligated to obey the whole law.* ***You who are trying to be justified by the law*** *have been alienated from Christ; you* ***have fallen away from grace****.*

> *James 2:10 - For whoever keeps the whole law and yet* ***stumbles at just one point is guilty of breaking all of it****.*

> *Romans 14:23b ESV - For* ***whatever does not proceed from faith is sin****.*

All of this is to say that sin is no longer the issue of our righteousness. Faith is! By faith, we have the righteousness of Jesus as a free gift and, therefore, we have access to God and all of His blessings, including healing, that otherwise would never be available to us.

Romans 3:22-24 - This ***righteousness is given through faith in Jesus Christ to all who believe****. There is no difference between Jew and Gentile, for all have sinned and fall short of the glory of God, and* ***all are justified freely by his grace*** *through the redemption that came by Christ Jesus.*

Romans 5:1-2 - Therefore, since we have been ***justified through faith****, we have peace with God through our Lord Jesus Christ, through whom we have* ***gained access by faith into this grace*** *in which we now stand. And we boast in the hope of the glory of God.*

Colossians 1:21-23a - Once you were alienated from God and were enemies in your minds because of your evil behavior. ***But now He has reconciled you by Christ's physical body through death to present you holy in His sight, without blemish and free from accusation-- if you continue in your faith****, established and firm, and do not move from the hope held out in the gospel.*

For us to consider that we attain our healing from God because we are doing good things or are not doing evil things means that we have shifted our attention to the knowledge of good and evil rather faith in Jesus' sacrifice. For us to think we can attain God's promises in our own striving and strength instead of simple faith in Jesus makes us just like the Israelites who thought they could conquer the Promised Land without God's power. If this is the case, then the evil one has deceived us into religion, legalism, and performance-based spirituality, which is essentially the same thing the serpent did when he persuaded Adam and Eve to eat from the forbidden tree when they already had everything they needed from God.

All of this is to say that since the beginning of mankind, only those with no knowledge of good and evil and childlike faith are able to freely receive the promises of God. This is no different for us as followers of Jesus.

Matthew 18:3 - And he said: "Truly I tell you, unless you change

> *and* ***become like little children****, you will never enter the kingdom of heaven."*
>
> *Mark 10:15 - "Truly I tell you, anyone who will not receive the kingdom of God* ***like a little child*** *will never enter it."*

This means that we receive from God according to what we truly believe Jesus did for us.

Faith in His Sacrifice

When Jesus walked the earth, He worked so many miracles for people that crowds followed Him from town to town, hoping to touch Him and be healed. At one point, when the crowds had it in their minds to force Him to be their King, He pointed out that they only loved Him because He worked miracles for them. They had become presumptuous in thinking it was easy for God to bless them freely. Jesus turned and admonished them for their lack of true understanding of His Kingdom. Then, He delivered His most challenging teaching to them by detailing what is required of those who follow Him and call Him their King. This is what He said:

> *John 6:53-57 - Jesus said to them, "Very truly I tell you, unless you eat the flesh of the Son of Man and drink His blood, you have no life in you.* ***Whoever eats My flesh and drinks My blood has eternal life,*** *and I will raise them up at the last day. For My flesh is real food and my blood is real drink.* ***Whoever eats My flesh and drinks My blood remains in Me****, and I in them. Just as the living Father sent me and I live because of the Father, so* ***the one who feeds on Me will live because of Me****."*
>
> *John 6:63 NLT - The Spirit alone gives eternal life.* ***Human effort accomplishes nothing****. And the very words I have spoken to you are spirit and life.*

To the mostly Jewish crowds following after Jesus, the proposal of drinking blood and eating flesh was completely preposterous heresy against God's Law and totally in contrast to anything the Messiah of the God of Israel would ever command His followers to do. Moreover, under the Law, they were accustomed to a relationship with God where God required strenuous obedience to a high standard of purity and holy conduct in order to earn His blessings. Therefore, after Jesus said these things, almost everyone who had been following Him murmured, grumbled against Him, and then abandoned Him. They no longer believed He was the Messiah.

Jesus did this on purpose. Claiming to follow Him and calling Him our King when our motives are self-serving only proves that we do not understand the price Jesus paid for us to be saved, healed, delivered, and sustained by Him. In order for us to receive blessings and benefits freely by grace, Jesus gave up everything, even His life. We follow a crucified King. In fact, on the night of Passover before He went to the cross, Jesus taught His disciples how to eat His flesh and drink His blood.

> *Matthew 26:26-28 - While they were eating, Jesus took bread, and when He had given thanks, He broke it and gave it to His disciples, saying, "**Take and eat; this is My body**." Then He took a cup, and when He had given thanks, He gave it to them, saying, "**Drink from it, all of you. This is My blood of the covenant, which is poured out for many for the forgiveness of sins.**"*

In the same way that the Jews observe Passover every year to remember how God delivered them from Egyptian slavery, followers of Jesus take Communion to remember Jesus' sacrifice and how God delivered us from the Law of sin and death.

In fact, when the Apostle Paul wrote to the Corinthian believers, he corrected some egregious sin in their church. However, he never said they were weak, sick, and dying because of sin. The Corinthians had excellent understanding of the absolute freedom we have from the condemnation of the Old Covenant Law. While Paul appreciated their grasp of Christian liberty, he corrected them for presumptuously abusing God's grace to pursue their own lusts, which was not beneficial for them or for others. (see 1 Corinthians 6:12, 8:1, 10:23) However, Paul did express clearly that some of the Corinthians were weak, sick, and dying because they were abusing the body and blood of Jesus by not properly honoring His sacrifice when they took Communion. Taking Communion renders judgment on everyone who partakes of it—condemnation for those who do not believe Jesus and blessing for those who do. Therefore, it was lack of true faith in Jesus' atoning sacrifice that caused some of them to fall into weakness, sickness, and death. Needless to say, Paul encouraged the Corinthians to examine their faith before taking Communion in order to be certain that they were partaking of the sacrifice of Jesus with due reverence for all He has done for us.

I Desire Mercy

When Jesus laid down His life for us, He was motivated by His great love for God and for us. Jesus loves us freely and fully, never brings up our past sins and mistakes, never holds a grudge or keeps us in a state of probation for bad behavior, and does not even demand anything from us to show Him our appreciation. Actually, many of Jesus' miracles and dealings with people were directly attributed to His great compassion.

> *Matthew 14:14 - When Jesus landed and saw a large crowd,* ***He had compassion on them and healed their sick.***

> *Matthew 20:34 -* ***Jesus had compassion on them*** *and touched their eyes. Immediately they received their sight and followed Him.*

> *Mark 6:34 - When Jesus landed and saw a large crowd,* ***He had compassion on them****, because they were like sheep without a shepherd. So He began teaching them many things.*

> *Mark 8:2 -* ***"I have compassion for these people****; they have already been with Me three days and have nothing to eat." (Then Jesus miraculously fed 4,000 men, plus women and children.)*

> *Luke 7:12-14 - As He approached the town gate, a dead person was being carried out--the only son of his mother, and she was a widow. And a large crowd from the town was with her.* ***When the Lord saw her, His heart went out to her*** *and He said, "Don't cry." Then He went up and touched the bier they were carrying him on, and the bearers stood still. He said, "Young man, I say to you, get up!"*

As His followers and participants in the New Covenant, Jesus gave us only one command. What we truly believe in our hearts about what Jesus has done for us is evidenced by our genuine compliance with His one command. (see James 2:17-18) This is His command:

> *John 13:34-35 - "**A new command I give you: Love one another. As I have loved you, so you must love one another**. By this everyone will know that you are My disciples, if you love one another."*

> *John 15:12-17 - "**My command is this: Love each other as I have loved you**. Greater love has no one than this: to lay down one's life for one's friends. You are My friends if you do what I command. I no longer call you servants, because a servant does not know his master's business. Instead, I have called you friends, for everything that I learned from My Father I have made known to you. You did not choose Me, but I chose you and appointed you so that you might go and bear fruit--fruit that will last--and so that whatever you ask in My name the Father will give you. **This is my command: Love each other.**"*

Without faith in Jesus, it is absolutely impossible for anyone to fulfill His one New Covenant command. Without faith in Jesus, we do not have the Holy Spirit and without the Holy Spirit, we will be unable to love the way Jesus did. In order to truly love the way Jesus loves, we must do something that our old Adamic nature is completely incapable of doing. We have to do the most selfless and costly thing we could ever do—we have to forgive and show mercy to those who can never pay us back, those who do not deserve our love and kindness, and especially to those who have hurt and offended us. In fact, spiritual fruitfulness is entirely a matter of the heart and has nothing to do with how many people we serve, how well we preach, teach, or lead worship, how rich or poor we are, or how much we sacrifice for God and His Kingdom. Any of us could do any of these things with a whole host of wrong motives, including but not limited to aiming for recognition, revenge, success, expecting some form of repayment, or trying to earn a reward from God rather than being motivated by genuine love for God and for others.

> *Galatians 5:22-23 - But the **fruit of the Spirit is love, joy, peace, forbearance, kindness, goodness, faithfulness, gentleness and self-control**. Against such things there is no law.*

2 Peter 1:5-8 - For this very reason, make every effort to ***add to your faith goodness****; and to goodness,* ***knowledge****; and to knowledge,* ***self-control****; and to self-control,* ***perseverance****; and to perseverance,* ***godliness****; and to godliness,* ***mutual affection****; and to mutual affection,* ***love****. For if you possess these qualities in increasing measure, they will keep you from being ineffective and unproductive in your knowledge of our Lord Jesus Christ.*

Through His sacrifice, Jesus has forgiven us and released us from an astronomical and absolutely unpayable debt of sin and transgression against Him. Our debt to God is so large that He has every right to keep us locked up in prison forever without hope of ever attaining freedom. It is only because of His compassion for us that we have received mercy. Therefore, when others sin against us, hurt us, offend us, cause us harm, or owe us something, we must recognize that their debt to us is small by comparison to the mercy that we have received from God. When we truly understand this, forgiving others comes easily. If we do not understand the mercy that we have received from God, it can be difficult to forgive others and therefore, we put ourselves in jeopardy of losing what Jesus died to give us. (see Matthew 18:23-35)

Matthew 6:14-15 - "For ***if you forgive*** *other people when they sin against you,* ***your heavenly Father will also forgive you****. But* ***if you do not forgive*** *others their sins,* ***your Father will not forgive your sins****."*

Mark 11:24-25 - "Therefore I tell you, whatever you ask for in prayer, believe that you have received it, and it will be yours. And when you stand praying, if you hold anything against anyone, ***forgive them, so that your Father in heaven may forgive you your sins****."*

Luke 11:4a - ***Forgive us our sins, for we also forgive*** *everyone who sins against us.*

James, the leader of the Jerusalem church and the author of the Book of James, taught believers about living lives of genuine mercy in this way. Anyone trying to earn righteousness through keeping the Old Covenant or "royal" Law will find themselves unable to attain it and will be condemned. But in the New Covenant, we have a new law, which is one of absolute liberty and mercy because of the blood of Jesus. We will be judged by this law, not according to our sins, but according to how much mercy we have shown to others.

> *James 2:12-13 - **Speak and act as those who are going to be judged by the law that gives freedom**, because judgment without mercy will be shown to anyone who has not been merciful. **Mercy triumphs over judgment**.*

To be clear, let me reiterate that our sins are forgiven exclusively through the blood of Jesus and NOT through our ability to forgive. Particularly as we believe God for healing through faith in Jesus, we are not ill due to mercilessness. Unforgiveness is not able to keep us trapped in sickness. However, our unforgiveness may be evidence of our own lack of faith in God's mercy towards us and the right standing that we have with God as a free gift.

Therefore, as we examine our own faith for receiving God's benefits and healing, it is oftentimes the mercy we extend freely to others from our hearts that the best evidence of what we truly believe about what Jesus has done for us.

The Gospel is the Power

It is worth noting that if we do not receive our healing instantly, it does not mean that we have no faith, are not saved, will not go to heaven, or that our names are not written in the Lamb's Book of Life. Faith in one component of our lives does not automatically guarantee that we have faith in another area of God's blessings and goodness toward us. For example, we can have great faith in some areas of our lives like salvation, evangelism, God's material provision, spiritual gifts, and serving others but still come up short in the area of faith to receive our healing. Also, we sometimes easily receive supernatural healing from the Lord for one condition or ailment but struggle to receive even marginal improvement from Him for other illnesses or infirmities. In view of this, failure to receive healing does not mean we do not believe Jesus at all but it can be evidence of unbelief in our hearts pertaining to some aspect of what He has accomplished for us.

This said, receiving our healing is as simple as receiving our salvation. It is entirely by grace through faith in what Jesus has done for us through His death and resurrection. God loves us so much that He laid down His life to redeem us from all oppression and every cause of sickness. The Gospel of Jesus Christ ***is*** the power of God for our salvation/yeshua.

> *Romans 1:16-17 - For I am not ashamed of the gospel, because* ***it is the power of God that brings salvation to everyone who believes****: first to the Jew, then to the Gentile. For* ***in the gospel the righteousness of God is revealed--a righteousness that is by faith from first to last****, just as it is written:* ***"The righteous will live by faith****."*

This means that we can receive salvation, deliverance, healing, and sustenance and every other blessing Jesus died to give us through our childlike faith in what He has done for us. Therefore, instead of striving to be good for God or striving to produce faith that will merit His healing and blessings, our work is to simply trust in Jesus.

> *John 6:29 NLT - Jesus told them,* ***"This is the only work God wants from you: Believe*** *in the One He has sent."*

So, let us press on to attain everything Jesus attained for us so that we can hear Him say to us, "Child of God, your faith has healed you."

Receiving

Chapter Six
COMMUNION

One of the best things we can do as an act of faith to receive our healing is to take Communion. Personally, I take Communion regularly but never religiously and, in the event that I become ill, I take Communion for healing in the place of medicine or any other remedy.

Every year, Jews celebrate the Passover to remember how God delivered them from the bitter bondage of Egyptian slavery. In a similar way, we take Communion as a way of remembering that Jesus offered His body and shed His blood as the eternal Lamb of God who delivered us from sin so that we can have direct access to God and His blessings, including healing. Each and every believer in Jesus is a royal priest of God who is authorized to serve and receive Communion. (see 1 Peter 2:9) The earliest followers of Jesus took Communion every time they met together and had Communion elements readily available in their homes at all of their meetings for anyone to partake at any time they desired. This said, just like the original Passover was only for those who had been circumcised into the covenant, taking Communion is only for those who are in covenant with Jesus through faith in Him.

This is because when we take Communion, we are re-enacting God's judgment of sin through the sacrifice of His Son. For believers, this is a total release from sin to freedom as we remember Jesus' words, "It is finished!" God's judgment is now in our favor because our sins have been forgiven, we have been redeemed from the curse of the Law, and we have triumphed over death and the evil one forevermore! Hallelujah! However, for unbelievers, the act of taking Communion renders judgment and condemnation. Therefore, we cannot treat it lightly and unbelievers must be advised to abstain.

When Jesus demonstrated to His disciples how to take Communion in remembrance of Him, He said, "This *is* my body" and "This *is* my blood of the New Covenant, shed for the forgiveness of sins." He did not say, this *becomes* or this *represents,* but this ***is***, even though He had not yet gone to the cross. Therefore, when we take Communion, even in His absence, we do so as an act of faith that we are eating His flesh and drinking His blood and that by doing so we have the life of God in us. We cannot regard this carelessly. In fact, when Paul rebuked the believers at Corinth for abusing the Communion elements, it was because they were eating the bread casually as a meal, getting drunk on the wine, and treating the blood and body of Jesus as common instead of honoring it as holy. This is a sin against Him and, consequently, taking Communion without due reverence for or faith in Jesus' sacrifice led some of them to be weak, sick, and even die. (see 1 Corinthians 11:27-31)

For this reason, Paul exhorted everyone partaking of Communion to examine ourselves for the genuineness of our faith before eating the body and drinking the blood of Jesus. Accordingly, when we examine ourselves before taking Communion, we are NOT self-examining for sin but taking an honest appraisal of our FAITH that Jesus died for the forgiveness of all of our sins. Actually, the Biblical word used to describe this self-examination is not one used for negatively testing something in order to expose faults and failures but positive testing for genuineness, like a fine jeweler inspecting a diamond to confirm that it is real. Taking Communion is an act of faith. As if we are painting the blood of the Lamb on the doorposts of our hearts so that the destroyer cannot harm us, we take Communion believing that no matter what we may have done or not done, we are completely forgiven and have access to God because of the broken body and shed blood of Jesus. He is our living Yeshua—our salvation, deliverance, healing, and sustenance have all been paid for through His sacrifice. The question is, do we really believe this? Is our faith real?

Taking Communion

To take Communion at home or in a small group, purchase bread (preferably unleavened) and wine (or grape juice) and set them apart as holy. Pray a simple prayer to devote them to God such as, "In the name of Jesus, I bless and consecrate this bread and wine to God's service for the purpose of Communion." After you have set the elements apart like this, do not use them for any other purpose. They are consecrated to God and, from this point forward, they must be used for Communion or be destroyed without being used.

As you prepare to take Communion alone or with a group, take a moment of silence to be still before the Lord. Reaffirm your faith in Jesus' sacrifice and examine your faith in Him as your only Savior, Deliverer, Healer, and Sustainer. Praise and thank Him for what He has done for you. Be led by the Holy Spirit into prayer or anything else you may want to say to the Lord and also keep your spiritual ears open to anything the Lord may want to say to you.

Read the following passage of Scripture and/or any of the Gospel accounts of Jesus serving the Lord's Supper to His disciples.

> *1 Corinthians 11:23b-26 - The Lord Jesus, on the night He was betrayed, took bread, and when He had given thanks, He broke it and said, "This is my body, which is for you; do this in remembrance of Me." In the same way, after supper He took the cup, saying, "This cup is the new covenant in My blood; do this, whenever you drink it, in remembrance of Me." For whenever you eat this bread and drink this cup, you proclaim the Lord's death until He comes.*
>
> *See also: Matthew 26:26-28; Mark 14:7-25; Luke 22:14-30; John 13:21-30*

Take the bread and wine in your hands and pause for a moment to honor them as holy. You can use the Scriptures at the end of this chapter to help you to recognize and rightly discern what the body and blood of Jesus have done for us.

To take Communion as an act of faith for healing, use the following declarations to affirm your faith. Believe them in your heart and speak them out loud.

> *I believe that Jesus shed His blood for the forgiveness of all of my sins. I am totally and completely forgiven, righteous before God and it is His will for me to be in health.*
>
> *I believe that Jesus offered Himself as a sacrifice to give me full*

and unhindered access to God and all of His blessings, including healing.

I believe that when Jesus hung on a cross for me, He redeemed me from the curse of the Law which includes every form of sickness.

I believe that Jesus' body was pierced, crushed, and wounded so that my body can be healed, restored, and made whole.

I believe that Jesus died and was raised from the dead to triumph over the powers of darkness, the evil one, and even death. Unclean spirits must leave me right now in Jesus' name and never return. I am filled with the Holy Spirit as a child of God.

I believe that I am eating the flesh and drinking the blood of Jesus so that I have the life and vitality of God in me to give strength and health to my mortal body.

I believe that I was healed by the stripes of Jesus.

Then, take your time as you eat the bread and drink the wine in remembrance of Jesus' sacrifice and receive your healing! Do this as often as you like and rejoice in all that God has done for you.

Selection of Scriptures
BODY AND BLOOD OF JESUS

*1 Peter 2:24 - **"He himself bore our sins" in His body** on the cross, so that we might die to sins and live for righteousness; **"by His wounds you have been healed."***

*Romans 5:9 - Since we have now been **justified by His blood**, how much more shall we be saved from God's wrath through Him!*

*Ephesians 1:7 - In Him we have **redemption through His blood, the forgiveness of sins**, in accordance with the riches of God's grace...*

*Hebrews 9:14 - How much more, then, will the **blood of Christ**,* *who through the eternal Spirit offered Himself unblemished to God, cleanse our consciences from acts that lead to death, so that we may serve the living God!*

Hebrews 10:10 - And by that will, we have been made holy through the sacrifice of ***the body of Jesus Christ*** *once for all.*

Colossians 1:22 - But now He has reconciled you ***by Christ's physical body*** *through death to present you holy in His sight, without blemish and free from accusation...*

Hebrews 10:19-22 - Therefore, brothers and sisters, since we have confidence to ***enter the Most Holy Place by the blood of Jesus****, by a new and living way opened for us* ***through the curtain, that is, His body****, and since we have a great priest over the house of God, let us draw near to God with a sincere heart and with the full assurance that faith brings, having our hearts sprinkled to cleanse us from a guilty conscience and having our bodies washed with pure water.*

1 John 1:7 - But if we walk in the light, as He is in the light, we have fellowship with one another, and ***the blood of Jesus, His Son, purifies us from all sin.***

Revelation 12:11 - They triumphed over him ***by the blood of the Lamb*** *and by the word of their testimony; they did not love their lives so much as to shrink from death.*

John 6:53-57 - Jesus said to them, "Very truly I tell you, unless you eat the flesh of the Son of Man and drink His blood, you have no life in you. ***Whoever eats My flesh and drinks My blood has eternal life,*** *and I will raise them up at the last day. For* ***My flesh is real food and My blood is real drink. Whoever eats My flesh and drinks My blood remains in Me, and I in them****. Just as the living Father sent me and I live because of the Father, so* ***the one who feeds on Me will live because of Me****.*

Chapter Seven

Do You Want to Be Well?

When Jesus came to the pool of Bethesda, there was a multitude of invalids who were desperately hoping to receive a miracle in the waters of the pool. Jesus saw a man who had been lame for 38 years and asked him, "Do you want to be well?" This seems like a strange question because one would think it is obvious that a sick person would want to be well. However, the man's response is indicative of what many of us do rather than truly applying our faith. He whined and gave excuses for why he couldn't receive his healing. Jesus replied by giving him a command that would engage his faith so that he could receive his healing and proceed with his life as if he had never been ill. The man obeyed Jesus' command and was instantly healed. (see John 5:1-9)

When we truly want to receive our healing from Jesus, we must do whatever is required of us to align ourselves with Him and what He has done for us. This means listening to the Holy Spirit and following His promptings, even if we have to start doing certain things and stop doing other things. This could include the rearrangement of all of our priorities and every aspect of our lives, even if we thought our lives were already based on godly principles, good theology, and common sense. We do not live and will not be healed by principles, theology, or common sense. Principles are man-made notions of God's ways and how to put them into practice, but they have a tendency to stem from or turn into principalities that desire to rule over us and keep us in bondage to something from which Christ died to set us free. Theology is knowledge about God but too much of it can often prevent us from actually knowing God or engaging our faith to receive anything from Him. Common sense is the wisdom of this world and includes the "logical" things that are either good or bad for us, but this is nothing more than confidence in the knowledge of good and evil rather than faith in Jesus who is the source of life. As sons and daughters of God, we live by being led by the Holy Spirit and He will often tell us to do something that is completely contradictory to our common sense, the wisdom of this world, the advice of physicians and well-meaning friends, and some of the most popular teachings in the Church. The Holy Spirit leads us in simple faith in Jesus and the price He paid for us to be healed.

If we are sick because of sin, the Holy Spirit will tell us. Then we can repent, believe that Jesus shed His blood for us to be forgiven, and receive our healing as a free gift. It can be helpful to say out loud, "Thank you God that I am forgiven because of the blood of Jesus." Remember, Jesus did not go on sin hunts, point out sins, or demand confession of sins before healing anyone, so we do not need to become overly self-focused and self-scrutinizing. Our healing and forgiveness is a free gift through the blood of Jesus, and we do not earn it based on confession of sin or lack of sin in our lives. This said, Jesus did tell the man at the pool of Bethesda, "Stop sinning or something worse might happen to you." When repentance is genuine, our behavior reflects it. Sometimes, we are able to instantly receive healing through faith that our sins are totally forgiven, and other times it takes us a while for us to come into agreement with what God has done for us.

If we are sick due to the curse of the Law or generational curses, the Holy Spirit will tell us. Then, we can break the power of the curse through our faith in the fact that Jesus redeemed us from it. It can be helpful to say out loud, "By the blood of Jesus, I am redeemed and set free from every curse." We must also be careful about over-spiritualizing our infirmity with thoughts such as, "I have a stiff neck because I have been stubborn like a stiff-necked Israelite toward God." Instead, it is better to set our hearts to seek the truth and allow the Holy Spirit to renew our minds in order to give us deeper understanding that Jesus truly did take all of our punishment upon Himself. This can entail allowing the Holy Spirit to correct our wrong ideas about God and His love that are more rooted in our heritage, upbringing, past experiences, or culture and to replace our erroneous beliefs with His truth. Then, we will experience more and more freedom from the curse of the Law and generational curses, including receiving our healing. Sometimes, we can experience instant and noticeable release from the effects of the curse in our lives and, other times, it takes a while for the truth to permeate our lives and replace the lies that keep us in bondage.

If we are sick due to demonic oppression, the Holy Spirit will tell us. Then, we can take authority over unclean spirits and command them to leave us in the name of Jesus. If there are specific foul spirits that need to be addressed and expelled, we can ask the Holy Spirit to help us to discern the spirits and He will tell us. Otherwise, any spirit that is not the Holy Spirit can be commanded and addressed as an "unclean spirit" or a "demon." While we do not want to become paranoid about demons or overly focused on evil, they are real and they are still the cause of some illnesses and addictions today. Therefore, when we are sick, it can be a good practice to command unclean spirits or even the name of the disease or affliction that is plaguing us to leave us in the name of Jesus. For example, we can say, "In the power and authority of the name of Jesus, I command cancer to leave my body right now and not return." When we stand in authority like this in the name of Jesus, which is above the name of every infirm condition, we can experience real and lasting results.

If we are sick due to unbelief in the finished work of Jesus, then we must spend time doing anything that builds our faith and stay away from things that foster our unbelief. We will cover this more in another chapter.

Not Wanting to Be Well

In some cases, knowingly or unknowingly, people do not actually want to be well. Even if they ask for prayer and verbally express their desire to be healed, there is something deeper going on beneath the surface that they may or may not be aware of. Their actions often reveal different priorities than they profess with their mouths. Or, even if their actions seem right, there are many mindsets people become trapped in which cause it to be very difficult, if not impossible, to receive anything from God. I am not suggesting that you suffer from any of the following mindsets or that you should go out suspecting and condemning sick people for not wanting to be well. However, addressing them can aid our own repentance, help us to help others receive their breakthrough, and prevent us over exerting ourselves with people who are not ready to be well yet.

Some people have come to prefer the special attention and treatment they receive for not feeling well or enjoy the things people do for them when they are in a weakened state. Others have made complaining a way of life and revel in pouting or mocking themselves and their infirmities in order to receive attention from other people. The attention they receive causes them to feel loved and appreciated and they begin to prefer sickness to health rather than humbling themselves before God in order to receive healing.

In situations where someone is being overworked, taken advantage of, or abused, they may invite or over-dramatize sickness because it is the only way they are able to take a break. Rather than being led by the Holy Spirit into true Kingdom service and having a backbone in their identity as a child of the Most High God, they use illness as a form of temporarily withdrawing from life. Then, once they are ready to be well, they become well again and continue with the way things were before. Others truly work themselves to exhaustion to the point where disease comes into their bodies. This type of overwork is usually rooted in fear and pride, and is not from the Lord.

Some people have simply struggled with infirmity and chronic pain or illness for so long they have given up, grown weary, fallen in a spiritual rut, or given way to believing that sickness is God's will for them rather than contending in faith at the direction of the Holy Spirit for the healing Jesus died to give them. There are also those who enjoy being sick because they feel closer to God when they are in a state of infirmity. This may be true but unfortunately, this is a perverted way of seeking God's Fatherly love and attention.

Other people point to other graces that God works in their lives while they are sick as proof of God's blessing upon them in spite of the fact that they are not receiving their healing from Him. For example, they will point out that because of their sickness, they have learned so much about God or that doors of evangelism were opened for them to people that they otherwise would not have reached. Although this causes them to appear very godly, it actually diverts their attention and yours away from their lack of faith for healing. It is true that God is so good that He works ALL things for our good when we trust in Jesus, including our sicknesses, and even our sins, errors, mistakes, and faithless moments. However, pointing to God's goodness should be an encouragement for believing Him more in every area of our lives rather than being used as a mask for our unbelief.

Some people are so afraid of being sick that they deny illness or are determined to conquer it in their own strength rather than letting God be their God by admitting their weakness and genuinely acknowledging their need for a Savior. Others are afraid of being made well because they don't think they would know how to proceed with life as a healed person, which is also self-reliance rather than trusting in Jesus to guide them through every turn of life.

Others are so busy and have filled their lives with so many things to do that they use this as an excuse for trusting in just about anything but God to sustain them so they can continue to live their lives the way they want to and maintain their busy schedule. They often say things like, "I have to take care of my family," or "I have to go to work to make money," as justifications for not actually trusting that God loves their family more than they do and is a better provider than they are. Not to put too fine a point on it, but in essence they are saying something along the lines of, "I can't trust God for my healing because I don't trust Him as my Provider." I have never heard anybody say this, but at least it would be honest. God can work with honesty. Unfortunately, their excuses only reveal unbelief upon unbelief when God's will for them is to move from faith to faith and glory to glory. It would be better for these people to seek the Lord and reassess their activities one by one based on whether or not the Lord truly initiated and desires to sustain the things that they are doing. This is why the subtlest of this kind are those who contend that they are busy because they are serving the Lord. For example, a man named Epaphroditus almost died of illness doing the work of the Lord because he overworked in order to make up for other people's lack of service. (see Philippians 2:29) However, when the Lord has truly appointed someone to do something, the Holy Spirit makes it easy, does not lead them into overwork, and supplies the needed strength and sustenance to complete God's purpose.

Some people will simply not do what is required of them to receive healing from God. Even if it outwardly appears they are living a very righteous life or that they have gone the distance to be touched by God, sometimes there is just a persnickety pride issue that prevents them from being able to do what God says. Only God knows the heart, but oftentimes people in this predicament would be willing to do something dramatic as an exhibition of their faithfulness, yet they refuse to do the one small or private thing that the Holy Spirit has asked them to do. Therefore, they miss out on what God has for them. For example, in the Old Testament, there was a man named Namaan who was a commander of the Syrian army and noted as a great man. But, Namaan was a leper. Namaan heard about Elisha the prophet of Israel who was able to cure him of his leprosy, so he traveled a long distance with silver, gold, and gifts of clothing. Elisha took none of Namaan's money and did not even meet with Namaan himself but sent a messenger to tell him to wash in the Jordan River seven times so that he would be clean and be healed. Namaan was insulted and went away in a rage. Namaan thought Elisha was going to come out personally to serve him by praying to God for him, and he also rejected the idea that the rivers in Israel were any better for washing than the rivers in Syria. Fortunately for Namaan, his servants stopped him from discarding God's instructions and forfeiting his healing. They said to him, "If the Lord had told you to do some great thing, would you not have done it? So you should obey this simple thing when He says wash and be healed!" Namaan washed in the Jordan River seven times and was completely healed of his leprosy to the point that his skin was like a baby's. (see 2 Kings 5)

God is love and love died to heal us. But, love also gives us free will to choose God's way or our own way. We have to recognize the difference between our own urgent yearning to be relieved of discomfort, infirmity, and inconvenience and the genuine desire to be healed by God. If we are too afraid to trust God, think we know better than God and His methods, enjoy sickness more than health, have more important things to do than follow His guidance, or aren't willing to do what He asks of us in order to be healed, then He will let us have our own way. But if we sincerely humble ourselves before Him, allow Him to be God to us, and trust Him to be our Healer based only on what Jesus did and not on anything that we have done, are doing, or ever will do to earn God's good graces, then He will heal us as a free gift by grace through faith.

In Real Life

Soon after the Lord asked me to renounce medicine, one of the first things He healed for me was headaches. Because my headaches were debilitating, lie-down-with-your-eyes-and-ears-covered headaches, at the first inkling of a headache coming on, I typically went straight to the medicine bottle before the pain became overly intense. But, when I committed to trusting Jesus completely for healing, I meant it. The first headache after this came on like a beast, and it was on a day when I had some important things to do. I was in too much pain to pray out loud so, instead, I fixed my thoughts on Jesus and believed in my heart that He paid in full for my healing. Because I know that Jesus is not religious about anything, I knew that at any point in time, I could take a pill to relieve my suffering and get on with my important day. The temptation to take the pain relief was very real, but the revelation of no condemnation if I did resort to pills gave me freedom and strength to trust Jesus exclusively. Even so, I had whirling thoughts about all the things I had to do and how I could not afford to have a headache on this day. Then, I realized afresh that Jesus is Lord and He knows how to accomplish His purposes in the earth with or without me. I said to Him, "Lord Jesus, this day is yours. I give it to you. Whether you take my headache away or I am lying in bed until tomorrow, I will do whatever Your will is for me. I am going to rest in faith that You know what is best for me, and You will show me what to do." These were not just words. I truly and totally gave up my plans and put myself entirely in the hands of the Lord. Within about thirty minutes, I arose from my bed with no headache. This same thing happened a few more times with the same results until finally, I received permanent breakthrough and have not had a headache, large or small, ever since. Thank you, Jesus! Hallelujah!

It was not God's will for me to have headaches. It is not God's will for you to be ill. It is God's will for you to be well. Do you want to be well?

Chapter Eight

ACCORDING TO YOUR FAITH

At one point during Jesus' ministry, two blind men followed Him crying out to Him for mercy. He stopped and asked if they believed He was able to heal them. When they affirmed their belief, Jesus said, "According to your faith, let it be done to you." (see Matthew 9:27-29) Their sight was completely restored. On another occasion, a Centurion came to Jesus on behalf of his dying servant and Jesus said, "Let it be done just as you have believed." His servant was totally healed. (see Matthew 8:13)

We receive from God what we truly believe Jesus has done for us. If we believe God is our Provider, then we experience His supernatural provision according to our faith. If we believe God is our Deliverer, then we experience God's unexplainable hand of deliverance in our lives according to our faith. If we believe God is our Healer, then we receive miraculous healing from Him according to our faith. If we partially believe God, or believe God for some things and not others, then we partially receive from God just as we have believed.

When Jesus chastised His disciples for being of *little faith*, the word He used does not actually mean small or tiny in the same way that we interpret little. It means *not trusting enough* or *not having enough confidence*. It was not that Jesus' disciples did not trust Him at all—of course they did! They had dropped everything in their lives to follow the man they believed to be the Messiah. They had seen Him work countless miracles right in front of them, and eventually they had even worked miracles in His name. It was only in certain scenarios that they did not trust Him or believe in His love enough to attain results.

God does not require great or gigantic faith from us in order to heal us. He is looking for pure faith. Jesus said that faith as small as a mustard seed can move a mountain. But, this mustard seed is not a hybrid mix with other garden plants. Our faith cannot be in Jesus plus anything else—just Jesus. The Apostle Paul made it his aim to know nothing except Jesus Christ, the One that was crucified, so that his faith and the faith of all followers of Christ would not be in anything other than the power of God. (see 1 Corinthians 2:2, 5)

Pure faith is simple trust in God. This trust goes much deeper than God's existence, abilities, power, or authority over all creation as His means of healing us. These are good and true things about God to believe. However, real faith goes deep down to our trust in God's nature. God is love. His love demolishes all of our fears of condemnation and punishment. His love removed every obstacle that stands in the way of us receiving every blessing from Him. His love pours out endless streams of mercy and compassion. His love heals us in our hearts, our souls, and our bodies.

Because of what Jesus did for us, sin, the curse of the Law, and the devil are no longer the problem and neither are ongoing pain and chronic infirmity. Fear and unbelief are the problem. When we are in faith, we do not deny pain or illness as some are in the habit of doing, but we do not allow pain or illness to move us into a state of fear. Fear is the opposite of faith. Fear, stress, and anxiety are symptoms of unbelief in God's love, rest, and peace that He freely gives us when we trust in Jesus. Medical reports, internet searches, talking with others who suffer from similar problems, and hearing stories about those who died from the condition that we also have are not helpful activities for building faith. We can spare ourselves the time because the evidence is conclusive—disease leads to death. We only think that we find it helpful to have more knowledge of the problem because we have grown so accustomed to a diet of the knowledge of good and evil. We convince ourselves that *knowledge is power,* but this is the lie that the devil has been selling from the beginning. Only knowledge of God through faith in the Lord Jesus Christ multiplies His power, grace, peace, and healing in our lives. (2 Peter 1:2)

Therefore, when it comes to believing God for healing, it is important that we understand that it is no longer a matter of will God heal or won't God heal. God HEALED two thousand years ago when His Son died on a cross and was raised from the dead. By His stripes, we ***were*** healed. This is in the past tense. In the same way that Jesus saved our souls through His death and resurrection but it took us some time to realize this and come into alignment with believing it in order for us to receive our salvation, Jesus healed us at the cross and we must allow the Holy Spirit to renew our minds until we believe it and receive healing in our bodies.

All of this is to say that, as a child of God, we don't have to struggle or beg for healing as if it is something God may be withholding from us. We can simply believe God and receive it. The Centurion did not beg Jesus to heal his servant but, rather, recognized the simplicity of Jesus' authority to give a command and have it fulfilled. (see Matthew 8:8) The Syrophoenician woman came to Jesus begging at first and He ignored and rebuked her. At this, her begging changed into faith and then Jesus granted her request. (see Matthew 15:27) The blind beggars we referenced at the beginning of this chapter went to Jesus begging at first, but He called them to a higher place than begging by deliberately confirming their faith.

God is not moved by begging, groveling, false attempts at humility and self-deprecation, or grandiose gestures of piety and faithfulness. He is not moved by our promises to be good, to serve Him, or to give to His Kingdom as if He needed anything from us or as if the work of Jesus is incomplete in any way. If we really meant these things, we would already be doing them. If we think God will be moved with compassion for our situation if we pray the right prayer, have the right person pray, or have a lot of people praying the same thing, then we have completely missed the point of what Jesus did for us.

God is not the one who needs to move. God moved two thousand years ago when He gave His Son as an all-sufficient sacrifice for everything we will ever need for every trial we will ever face between now and when we go to heaven. God did a perfect work. Jesus said, "It is finished." The Holy Spirit's job is to teach us and remind us of this as our present truth. Our healing comes when we simply trust God, move ourselves out of His way, and receive the health that is His will for us.

Jesus taught us to pray to our Father in Heaven, "Your Kingdom come, Your will be done, on earth as it is in heaven." We do not have to chase after the Kingdom or the power of God or every new wind of teaching that passes through the Church. In fact, doing so only reveals our immaturity and will most likely lead to fatigue, burn out, false hope, religious acts, and possibly deception. (see Ephesians 4:14) The Kingdom of God dwells within us. (see Luke 17:21) The same power that raised Christ from the dead is inside us to equip and empower us to receive everything Jesus died to give us. (see Romans 8:11; Ephesians 1:19-22)

Actually, what takes the greatest faith of all is to repent and put our trust wholeheartedly and unreservedly in Jesus and His sacrifice for us as the greatest demonstration of God's love for us. The word for repentance the New Testament Greek means *change your mind* and the Old Testament Hebrew word for repentance means *to turn around*, implying a total change of direction in our actions. To say that we believe God but continue to trust in anything or anyone but God is not real repentance. We can say that we believe all sorts of things, but what we really believe is evidenced by the actions that we take to put our beliefs into action by placing our lives in God's hands and allowing Him to have His way with us. Accordingly, a prayer of repentance is not necessarily real repentance. God knows if we are honoring Him with our lips but far from Him in our hearts. (see Isaiah 29:13; Matthew 15:8) The Apostle Peter told people to "repent and turn to God." This has two parts. The first part is to stop trusting in what you have been believing and the second part is to start trusting in Jesus. (see Acts 3:19) In a similar fashion, God told Isaiah to keep preaching the truth to people no matter what because, at any point, if they were willing, they could repent, turn to Him and be healed. (see Isaiah 6:10) This is still true for us today whenever we are willing to repent and turn to God.

While it can build faith to read the stories of the characters in the Bible and how they received healing by faith, we must be careful not to focus too much on them and what they did. This is because even though reading the Word of God and these miracle stories can build faith, it does not take great faith to imitate a Bible character and pantomime a re-enactment of their healing to try to attain the same results that they did. Plus, this has the potential to lead us into trying to use techniques or methods which are nothing more than attempts to manipulate God into giving us what we want. This is religion, not faith. It can also lead us into having faith in our own faith, meaning our ability to procure or achieve a certain state of faith, which is turning faith into a work. This is flesh, and will profit nothing.

Instead, it is best to focus on Jesus who is the prime example of the life of a son or daughter of God, filled with the Holy Spirit, living in a tent of flesh, trusting God without reservation. Jesus was never sick and He believed God, His loving Father, so much that all things were possible to Him. At the same time, He humbled Himself before God to such a degree that He could do nothing by Himself. (see John 5:19, 30) Utter helplessness in our own strength is the place of total faith in God. But few of us worship God enough to be willing to humble ourselves before Him to this degree.

Significantly, the primary word used to describe healings in the New Testament is *therapueuo*, from which we derive our word therapy. Sometimes we receive instantaneous healing from God and we should never stop believing for this. But, do we trust God enough to humble ourselves before Him and let Him perform therapy on us? Interestingly, this word can also mean *to wait upon God* or *to worship*. Do we believe in God's healing enough to offer our bodies to Him and depend upon Him as our New Testament form of worship? Do we trust in God's love enough to wait upon Him, obey His voice, allow Him to have His way in our lives, and show Himself to be our Healer?

Real Faith

One of the best things we can do is to honestly assess and admit the condition of our faith. If we are struggling with little faith or it is obvious that we are not receiving God's blessings and benefits in a certain area of our life, it is only when we are honest about it that we can press onward from where we are and allow God to renew our minds into deeper levels of trust. If the Apostle Paul can admit that he had not attained the fullness of all that Jesus died to give us, then it's safe for us to admit that we might be falling short in a few areas of believing. (see Philippians 3:12-13) Here are some questions that may help you to assess your ability to receive your healing according to your faith.

Do you believe that God exists? This is a good start. This means that you have a measure of faith.

Do you believe God is able to heal you? This means that you have a measure of faith for healing. However, God probably seems distant and unpredictable, as if God may randomly choose to heal you someday if He feels like it. You may also have doubts about Jesus being the only Savior of mankind and the only way to access God's blessings of heaven.

Do you believe that your healing from God is conditional, based on an "If I..., then God will..." type of requirement? Unfortunately, this is not faith in God but in your own righteousness and is also known as religion. If there is something you have to do or stop doing in order to be healed, then you do not actually believe that healing is yours for free because of Jesus' finished work.

Do you believe that God will heal you? For example, sometimes when people believe God for healing, they say things like, "I know that God *is going to* heal me" or "I am *expectant* for healing." Unfortunately, this is not faith. This is hope. The Biblical word for *hope* means *confident expectation of receiving something in the future*. God is not going to heal you, He DID heal you. If you keep expecting that God is going to heal you in the future, then your healing will remain in the future because you do not actually believe that Jesus healed you at the cross two thousand years ago.

Do you believe that God healed you at the cross? This is actual faith in the finished work of Jesus. This is accurate revelation of the truth of what He did for us. You will know that you truly believe this in your heart when you are free from fear, confusion, condemnation, religion, and distant expectation. Even so, you may still struggle to receive the benefits that you believe have been made freely available to you.

Do you believe that because of Jesus, healing is already yours? This is the type of faith that steps into the promise of healing and receives the substance of it as evidence that it is true for us right now. (see Hebrews 11:1) You will know you have this kind of faith because your body is literally, physically healed.

Along these lines, it is a good practice to put our faith for healing into effect by doing something as an act of faith though it seems contradictory to our condition. This is not an act of denying our infirmity but a demonstration of our belief that Jesus took our infirmity upon Himself. For example, Jesus told a man with a withered hand to stretch it out, something that had been impossible for him before. His hand was not healed before he stretched it out but while he stretched it out. (see Matthew 12:13) When Jesus, Peter, and Paul told lame men who had never walked to stand up and walk as if they had never not walked, the men were healed when they put their faith into action and obeyed. (see Mark 2:11; Acts 3:6, 14:9) When Jesus told the ten lepers to go show themselves to the priests, they did not receive their healing in the presence of Jesus but *as they went*. (see Luke 17:14) When Jesus told the nobleman that his son would live and not die, he *took Jesus at His word* and demonstrated faith by returning home. (see John 4:50) Their faith was revealed by their actions.

Sometimes the Holy Spirit directs us into specific acts of faith, and other times we knowingly or unknowingly create rules in our own minds for what we need to do in order to receive our healing from God. For example, the woman with the issue of blood had created terms in her mind that she had to touch Jesus' garment in order to be healed. Even though God had not put forth any such stipulation, she was in faith and received her healing when this self-made requirement was fulfilled and it was done for her according to her faith. This said, I do not recommend haphazardly creating rules like this for ourselves because God is not obligated in any way by our self-induced mandates. The point is for us to step out of hope and into faith, and to keep on testing out various acts of faith until our healing manifests. Abraham, the father of the faith, did not waver from believing the promise of God or in God's ability to fulfill His word, even though his circumstances appeared completely contradictory to everything God had said. He continued to live his life as if God's promises were true until they came to pass just as God had promised. (see Romans 4:20) In the same way, we must each put our own faith into practice and live as a healed person.

In addition to this, we cannot treat our walk of faith as if it is a walk with a psychologist rather than a Savior, Deliverer, and Healer. Jesus did not come to die on a cross, be raised from the dead, ascend to heaven, and pour out the Holy Spirit so that we could do endless self-inspections to uncover our past hurts and offenses and how they have shaped our lives. At His death, Jesus did not say, "It is a work in progress," but instead said, "It is finished!" No matter what events may have caused us harm or damaged our hearts and minds, if the offenses took place in the past, are occurring in the present, or happen in the future, the repentance we enter into as we walk with Jesus is one of bringing everything in our lives into alignment with the fact that He did a perfect work. If we have sinned, we must receive His forgiveness and move on with our lives by obeying His voice. If others have sinned against us, we must forgive them and move on with our lives by obeying His voice. When we do this, our lives will no longer be shaped by our past or our wounds but by the finished work of Jesus and by fulfilling His purpose for us in His Kingdom. More significantly, we will receive full healing for our all of our mental, emotional, psychological, and physical wounds as if we had never been hurt.

We must also be careful about abusing God's love, grace, and mercy for us to comfort ourselves in our lack of repentance. We do this when we say things like, "I have been wounded and God knows that it is hard for me," or, "God knows my weakness and He loves me anyway." Yes, God does love us but if His lovingkindness is truly at work in our lives, then it will lead us into deeper repentance and trust in Jesus for our salvation, deliverance, healing, and sustenance. (see Romans 2:4; 2 Corinthians 7:10) The Christian life is not about being broken in our sin but being broken from our sin. In fact, for us to profess faith in Jesus without aligning our lives with what He did for us is hypocrisy, vanity, and self-deception. Faith in a God who enables false dependencies of our flesh is a perversion of the Gospel of Jesus Christ, who died on a cross for us to blot out our past, give us heaven on earth, and set us free from reliance on anything but Him. Instead of distorting God's love and mercy to settle for less than Jesus died to give us, we must press into real faith until the Kingdom of God manifests in our lives on earth as it is in heaven. The mature mindset of a Christian believer is to live in a way so as to continually press deeper and deeper into laying hold of God's unfathomable love for us as we place our trust wholeheartedly in Him. (see Philippians 3:15)

God is such a loving Heavenly Father that He is willing and able to work with us wherever we are on this spectrum of faith and regardless of whatever mistakes we may have made in our lives or our journeys of faith. Therefore, it is safe to admit little faith, lack of faith, or faith that has not yet matured to the point of receiving. As a matter of fact, if we genuinely humble ourselves before God by being honest with Him about ourselves, He will open doors to great blessings for us. He is not blocked from blessing us for any reason. However, if we think we are faith superstars who know it all, or that God delights to pander to our fleshly weaknesses, then God will most likely let us stay stuck in the same place for as long as we think so.

This said, while it is safe to admit little faith, it is never acceptable to judge anyone (including ourselves) for it. There is no condemnation for those who are in Christ Jesus, and that includes no condemnation for little faith. Blaming anyone for their inability to receive God's blessings is completely unhelpful and can do serious damage to the faith that they do have. Instead, we must encourage ourselves and one another in the faith, build one another up in the love and mercy of God, and set the example of trusting God in every aspect of our lives so that all of us can receive everything Jesus died to give us.

In Real Life

One summer, a torrential thunderstorm broke out in the middle of the day and I was rushing home because the person I was living with at the time had a dog that was terrified of this kind of weather. I pulled into the driveway and I knew I had to run quite a distance to get to the door. I was wearing very cute but very flimsy shoes. As I ran, I felt a pop in my calf muscle and knew that I had torn it. From my years of ballet training, I know what a torn muscle feels like so there was no mistaking it. I thought to myself, "This is going to take at least a few weeks to return to normal," and started to think about how this was going to impact the next several weeks of my life. I cried out to Jesus in pain. I knew that I was healed two thousand years ago on the cross, but unfortunately this injury was entirely my fault. He said, "I'm not holding it against you. Believe me for full healing." I said, "But it's really my fault." He said, "I'm not holding it against you. Believe me for healing." So, I set myself to believe that even things that are my fault are not counted against me and I carried on with my day the best that I could, not denying the pain that I was in but living as a healed person and walking as normally as possible as an act of faith. By that night, my muscle was completely healed with no pain. The next morning, I woke up and went to the gym as usual. Praise the Lord!

As another example, I have suffered from a skin disease since the age of thirteen. Over the years, before becoming a believer and after, I have tried every imaginable cream, prescription ointment, natural remedy, vitamin supplement, and nutritional or dietary regulations in order to be cured but none of them worked with any lasting results. As I walked deeper with the Lord, I tried every prayer technique and pursued every Christian teaching in the Church that might lead me to my healing. Several of these approaches blamed something from my past as the culprit for my continued condition which only caused me to focus on the past and perpetuate my ailment. While some of these methods brought about some short-term benefits, as time went on, my skin grew worse than it had ever been before. It was repulsive. Many times, I grew completely discouraged and weary in believing. Then one day, I looked at myself in the mirror and I said, "According to your faith, it is being done unto you." I realized that if my skin were evidence of my faith, then my faith was pretty weak. As discouraging as this sounds, there was no condemnation in it and it was the place of true humility. It was a turning point in my ability to receive healing for this condition. Since then, I have put all other techniques away and simply trust God. As I come into deeper understanding of His love for me and allow Him to remove all of my fear, guilt, and shame, I have watched my skin supernaturally improve right before my eyes. By the time you read this, there may be no evidence that I was ever plagued by this skin disorder. God is good, and He is good to us. Our work is to believe it.

Chapter Nine

HELP MY UNBELIEF

There was a man who brought his demon-possessed son to Jesus to have the demon cast out of him. Jesus' disciples had been unable to expel the demon, so at first the man said to Jesus, "If you can do anything...please help us." Jesus rebuked him for this assertion that anything was impossible for God and the man corrected himself, crying out, "I do believe; help my unbelief!" (see Mark 9:24) At this, Jesus commanded the evil spirit to leave the boy and he was completely healed. When Jesus' disciples asked Him why they had not been able to drive the demon out of the boy, He told them it was because of their unbelief. (see Matthew 17:20)

Unbelief prevents us from experiencing all of the blessings that are God's will for us, including healing. It occurs when we consider that our current circumstance is too difficult for God to handle or that our present problem has somehow not been addressed through the sacrifice and resurrection of Jesus. This said, the free gift of salvation, deliverance, healing, and sustenance is ours to receive by faith as long as we have the faith of Abraham, who believed that God raises the dead. (see Romans 4:16) The best part of this is that once we truly believe in our hearts that God can raise the dead, then every other problem becomes trivial by comparison. Every form of sickness, infirmity, plague, infection, and physical brokenness is a much smaller matter than death.

The Scriptures contain historical accounts of eight people in addition to Jesus who were raised from the dead by the power of God. Jesus raised three people from the dead during His ministry, Peter and Paul raised people from the dead, and Elijah and Elisha raised boys from the dead, in addition to a man whose dead body was disposed of by his travelling companions only to have it touch Elisha's corpse and be raised back to life by the power of God still resting on Elisha's bones. (see Luke 7:14, 8:53; John 11:43; Acts 9:40, 20:10; 1 Kings 17:22; 2 Kings 4:34)

Abraham had such complete confidence in God that he was willing to lay Isaac on the altar of sacrifice and slay him as an offering to God because he trusted that God was able to fulfill His promises, even if it required raising the dead. (see Genesis 22; Hebrews 11:19) Jesus trusted God so much that He laid down His own life and went to the cross because He believed that God would fulfill His Word.

All of this is to say that when we have real faith in God, even if it is only the size of a mustard seed, everything is possible to us. We stop fearing anything or even thinking things like, "If you can…" to God because we start to truly entrust ourselves into His hands as our loving Heavenly Father no matter how grim our circumstances may appear to be.

Types of Unbelief

There are various types of unbelief and enemy attacks against our faith that seek to thwart our ability to receive the blessings God has for us. Understanding them can be helpful in assessing the condition of our hearts.

Disbelief is the inability or refusal to believe or trust in something. Disbelief says things like, "I do not believe that Jesus heals today." Just because we do not believe something does not mean it is not true. This said, if we do not believe something that Jesus died to give us, then we will be highly unlikely to receive it from God unless He dramatically intervenes in our lives—which He has been known to do.

Unbelief in its simplest form is *weakness of faith* or *faithlessness*. It stems from the same word used for an unbeliever because it indicates that we think something is too impossible or too *unbelievable* to be real. This does not always mean we have no faith but that we have been stretched in our faith past our ability to believe or accept something. For example, unbelief says, "I know that Jesus died for my sins, but I'm not sure He can heal me." When we have varying levels of unbelief in our hearts, it is still possible to receive from God, but it will undoubtedly be inconsistent, unreliable, and feel more like a wrestling match than an easy flow of faith.

Misbelief is faith in something that is wrong. We have faith, but we have placed our faith in something that has no power to heal us. Believing in anything other than the finished work of Jesus' sacrifice and resurrection as the solution to any circumstance, trial, or apparent problem is a misbelief. For example, misbelief says things like, "Time heals all wounds." Time does not heal, Jesus heals. Misbeliefs are also the result of ideas, strategies, or teachings that support the belief that Jesus is not God, did not come in the flesh, did not die, was not raised from the dead, or is not King of the Universe. This type of misbelief says things like, "I believe Jesus was a good teacher like many other religious leaders." While it is possible for those with misbeliefs to procure some apparent results in their circumstances, the effects will prove to be temporary because misbeliefs will not yield salvation, deliverance, healing, or sustenance from the hand of God.

Self-righteousness is the most common and deadly misbelief. Simply put, self-righteousness is faith in our own record before God rather than in Jesus' perfect record. Self-righteousness says things like, "If I am a good person and do this or that, then God will heal me," or it may also say something like, "I deserve to be sick because I did something bad." Self-righteousness can surface as pride or as self-pity by saying things like, "I deserve to be blessed," or, "I'm not good enough for God to bless me," or it can whine with exasperation, "I am a good person, why won't God bless me?" It is possible to achieve some results through self-righteousness. A King named Hezekiah prayed a self-righteous prayer to God from his deathbed, asking God to heal him because of all the wonderful things he had done to serve God, and God added fifteen years to his life. (see Isaiah 38:3-4) This said, Hezekiah trusted God and had singlehandedly instituted massive reforms to abolish all forms of false worship from among God's people. No other king did as much as Hezekiah. (see 2 Kings 18:5) If you have a record like Hezekiah's, your self-righteousness may yield some results. But if you are like me, then standing on your own record before God will most likely result in weakness, disease, and possibly even death.

Psychologizing our faith is another prevalent misbelief. Psychologizing points us to inspect our past for reasons why we feel disconnected from God or are not experiencing the fullness of His blessings. This kind of misbelief says things like, "I was unloved by my father, so it is hard for me to believe that God is a loving Heavenly Father." Unfortunately, this is the wrong basis for faith in God altogether. God's love for us is not based on our past but on the sacrifice of His Son in order to adopt us as His children. Everything about the person we used to be died on the cross with Christ so that we can live as a new creation and receive all of God's blessings. Digging into our past is the enemy's tactic of bringing to remembrance the very things Jesus blotted off the record through the shedding of His blood. While it is possible to experience some healing and deliverance through the process of psychologizing, the Scripture says that we are transformed from glory to glory by beholding the glory of the Lord, not by beholding our own sin and brokenness. (see 2 Corinthians 3:18)

Unforgiveness is not the same as unbelief, but it can be evidence of unbelief. This said, Jesus never refused to heal someone because they had unforgiveness in their lives. The blood of Jesus provides such complete forgiveness for our sins that He is not holding our unforgiveness against us. However, if we are believing God for something like healing, we should not be surprised if opportunities to forgive others all of a sudden become prevalent in our life, including past wounds resurfacing and new offenses being inflicted by those around us. As we have covered in prior chapters, the state of our faith for receiving mercy from God is evidenced by how readily we extend mercy to those who hurt us.

Everything about this world, our flesh, and the evil one conspire to destroy the faith we have in the finished work of Jesus by creating doubt and presenting other seemingly viable alternatives for attaining the results we desire. The forces of darkness set themselves up to deny the salvation, deliverance, healing, and sustenance God provides for us through His Son, Jesus. (see 2 Corinthians 10:5; Ephesians 6:10-12) The enemy will do everything in his power to snatch real faith away from us before it has time to take root and to persecute real faith out of us through the mockery and rejection of others in unbelief, misbeliefs, or disbelief. If we endure through this, then the world magnifies its priorities by emphasizing our temporal need like food and clothing or by appealing to our selfish desire for comfort and satisfaction in order to distract us away from trusting in Jesus and staying on the narrow path of faith. (see Matthew 13:1-23)

The only way to demolish and overcome these agents of unbelief is to not trust in them or anything that they offer as a substitute for placing our faith exclusively in Jesus Christ and Him crucified. We prove all alternatives to be powerless by trusting in God alone, who raises the dead, and letting God's will be proven in our lives on earth as it is in heaven. Once we begin trusting in God and seeing Him work on our behalf, it becomes more challenging for the enemy to deceive us into false trusts.

Repent

In order to truly combat and conquer unbelief, misbelief, and disbelief, we must be willing to let go of everything we have ever thought to be true in order to be taught by the Holy Spirit. This will include challenging, refuting, and disproving common sense approaches of this world, beliefs that we were taught as a child, methods that may have worked for us in the past, and even some of the best known teachings in the Church. We have to allow the Holy Spirit to renew our mind, will, and emotions by demolishing our pride and our wrong ideas about God and His love for us.

In fact, Jesus taught that if our eye causes us to sin, we should pluck it out, and if our hand causes us to sin we should cut it off. (see Matthew 5:29-30) Even though Jesus often spoke in parables, He was not using hyperbole or exaggeration in this passage as much as we would like to think. When Paul taught about not indulging our own desires, he went further than Jesus had and instructed believers to consider ourselves completely dead to all of our body parts so that we could live as slaves to the perfect will of God. (see Romans 6:11-18) This is what repentance looks like and is part of what it means to take up our cross and follow Jesus by saying to God, "Not my will, but Yours be done."

Along these lines, some kinds of unbelief are only dealt with through prayer and fasting. To fast is to voluntarily submit ourselves to fleshly weakness by abstaining from eating food. Our flesh is an enemy of the Spirit of the Lord and fasting crucifies our flesh so that the power and voice of the Holy Spirit is magnified in our lives. (see Romans 8:6-8) True fasting is an act of worship. While we do not have time in this book to go into the details of fasting, there are many different types of fasts throughout the Scriptures. Jesus fasted for 40 days in the wilderness without food and came out endued with power from heaven for ministry and miracles. (see Luke 4:2, 14) Moses, Nehemiah, Esther, Daniel, David, and the people of Israel fasted as a demonstration of repentance and humbling themselves before God and in hope of God's presence and power. (see Exodus 24:18, 34; Nehemiah 1:4; Esther 4:16; Daniel 1:8, 10:2; 2 Samuel 12:16; 1 Samuel 7:6; Joel 1:14, 2:15; Leviticus 16:29) John the Baptist, his disciples, and Anna fasted in eager expectation of God fulfilling His promise. (see Luke 2:37, 5:33) Jesus made it abundantly clear that His disciples are called to fast and after He ascended to heaven, His earliest disciples fasted regularly. (see Matthew 9:15; Acts 13:3, 14:23) Perhaps if we fasted as diligently as the people in the Bible did, we would see the power of God's Spirit move the way that they did.

It is worth noting that Biblical fasting is fasting from food. While it is possible to abstain from all sorts of indulgences and activities that do not draw us closer to God, those are typically things we should probably not be doing anyway, so they tend to fall more into the category of things which should be reduced or cut out of our lives altogether.

Faith Comes by Hearing

Faith is generated when we hear the Good News of Jesus Christ. (see Romans 10:17) As such, the best way to build faith and dismantle all forms of unbelief is through the Word of God—the Scriptures. The Holy Spirit who dwells within us is the original author of the Word of God, so invite the Holy Spirit to help you while you read it, study it, meditate on it, memorize it, and read it some more. If you are unable to read for any reason, listen to someone else read it. As we hear the Word of God, we begin to be less conscious of the matters of this world and more focused on the matters of heaven, in the presence of God, where there is no sickness, death, mourning, crying, or pain.

The Word of God helps us to know God and trust in His love, goodness, and miracle working power and it is our safeguard against misbeliefs and wrong ideas about who God is. God upholds the universe by the word of His power, and we can live not by bread alone, but by His Word. (see Hebrews 1:3; Deuteronomy 8:3) This includes God's written Word and the prophetic words that God still speaks to and through each of us as His children. (see Acts 2:17-18) In fact, every word from the Spirit of the Lord has the power to build faith and also to give life. Older translation use the word *quicken,* which means to *revive, restore to life or health, preserve, cause to grow, recover, repair, make whole*, or *endue with greater power of life*. In Psalm 119, the Psalmist repeatedly asks God to quicken him or give him life according to His word. Throughout the New Testament, the Holy Spirit is credited as being the one that quickens us to life. (The list of Scriptures at the end of this book includes those pertaining to healing and quickening our bodies.)

Meditating on God's marvelous works and His faithfulness is another good way to build faith. (see Psalm 77:11-12, 119:27, 143:5, 145:5) These can be the miracles we read about in the Bible, but it can also include the ways God has intervened in our own lives to rescue, heal, and deliver us, and the testimonies of other believers who have experienced God's supernatural salvation, deliverance, healing, and sustenance in their lives. God's hand is still stretched out in the earth today to confirm the name of Jesus with healings, miracles, signs, and wonders. The story of God's faithfulness is not finished yet. The Book of Acts is still happening in the earth and can be the present reality of every follower of Jesus today.

Moreover, Jesus warned His disciples to be careful how we hear and what we listen to. (see Luke 8:18) Particularly when we believe God for healing in our bodies, we should be cautious about listening to anything that contradicts the Good News of Jesus or leads us deeper into doubt or unbelief rather than building our faith. If people spent as much time reading the Scriptures and researching real testimonies of God's power working miracles in people's lives as they did investigating their medical diagnosis and illnesses, then I guarantee their health would be dramatically different.

Help My Unbelief

Condemning, punishing, or rejecting someone for unbelief is like refusing to feed a starving person because they are hungry. This makes no sense. If a person is hungry, feed them. If a person is struggling with unbelief, they need to hear about what Jesus has done. This said, when we are struggling with various forms of unbelief, it is often difficult for us to see in ourselves what may be obvious to someone else. So, this next section is presented in the form of ministering to ourselves and to one another as fellow believers in Jesus.

In the event that unbelief is present, teach the truth of the finished work of Jesus. Teach them from the Scriptures about how Jesus conquered every enemy and solved every problem they will ever face for the rest of eternity. Share the Gospel stories of Jesus miraculously healing people. Testify to them of how God has worked in your own life or ask them to share a story of how God has been good to them. Use this as a baseline foundation for establishing and building faith to receive more and more of God's blessings. They believe—help their unbelief!

If someone is trapped in sin, proclaim the Gospel to them even if they are already a believer. Jesus died for us when we were sinners, enemies of God, and did not deserve mercy. He took all of our sin upon Himself and atoned for all of our sins past, present, and future so that there is now no condemnation for us. It is a lie to believe that sin in our life can block the healing power of God or that sin in our life "opens a door" to sickness. People who believe this go looking for sin around every corner and become paranoid about "what opened the door?" Whatever it was that may have opened the door, Jesus shut the door once and for all. Our job is to believe this. Going on sin hunts is something Jesus never did. Moreover, as His authorized ambassadors, our assignment is the ministry of reconciliation whereby we forgive sin and do not hold people's trespasses against them. (see John 20:23; 2 Corinthians 5:19) If they need to confess their sins, then let them and treat them gently with compassion and mercy. Make sure they know that their sins are totally and completely forgiven and help them to place their faith in the blood of Jesus.

If someone is in bondage to wrong beliefs or to fear, stress, or anxiety, then affirm them in the supremacy of Jesus, the love of God, and the rest and peace that we have because of what Jesus did for us. Ask for the Holy Spirit to reveal truth and increase His presence with them as their Comforter and Counselor who comes alongside them to guide them into every blessing God has for them. Be sure to tell them to obey whatever the Holy Spirit tells them to do. As believers in Jesus, we have authority over all creation, every unclean spirit, and even over our physical body as a created thing. Recognize the God-given authority that we have in the earth as His children and command unclean spirits to leave them or command their body parts to be healed in the name of Jesus. For example, speak out loud, "In the power and authority of the name of Jesus, I command fear, stress, and anxiety to leave and never return," or "Kidneys, be healed, in Jesus' name."

It can be helpful to try to discern which tactic the enemy is using to keep them stuck in unbelief. Without interrogating them, ask them questions about what is going on in their faith under the surface. Have they allowed faith to be snatched out of their heart? If so, help them recommit to trusting Jesus. Are they allowing the voices of other people to influence them more than the truth of the Gospel and the whisper of the Holy Spirit? If so, encourage them to spend some time alone in prayer, wait until they hear God speak to them, do what He tells them to do, and not to listen to anyone who contradicts what God said. Are they distracted by their temporal needs, or are they making choices based on the priorities of this world or comfort rather than purity of faith? If so, help them to count the cost of following a crucified King and encourage them to stop trusting in the ways of this world and be willing to let go of everything for the sake of seeing the Kingdom of God manifest in their life.

If someone continually presents their own goodness or obedience, even obedience to the Holy Spirit, as a reason they should be blessed, then they are trapped in self-righteousness. Remind them that we cannot earn or merit our healing from God for good behavior. A "bad" person who does horrible things can receive healing from God if they truly trust Jesus and not themselves whereas, a "good" person who strives to be pleasing to God on their own merits will struggle to receive anything from Him.

Use examples like this to dismantle their self-confidence and help them to trust in the blood of Jesus and not in their own efforts, methods, or worthiness.

It can also be helpful to inquire about any areas of unforgiveness in their lives as long as we remember that Jesus never refused to pray for anyone because they had unforgiveness in their hearts. If there is unforgiveness, ask God to pour out more mercy to them and to give them greater revelation of His mercy. Encourage them to stand in prayer, believing that they receive from God because of God's mercy for them through the blood of Jesus and at the same time encourage them to extend that mercy to others by forgiving everyone who has hurt them. (see Mark 11:26)

Avoid endorsing unbelief with sympathy and, if you the one who is sick, avoid those who comfort you too much or glorify you for continuing to praise God even though you have not been healed. Too much sympathy will keep you sick and may lead to your death. God is worthy of our praise because He is God. Being glorified in our unbelief will not help us to repent and be healed. Jesus did not heal with sympathy or comfort anyone in their condition. He stepped into action to bring the reality of heaven to earth. Sympathy comforts the flesh in all of its wrong ways of thinking and doing things and makes us feel better. Compassion crucifies the flesh. This does not always feel good, but it yields results from the power of the Holy Spirit. Sympathy says, "If I were sick, I would be sad." Compassion rejects excuses and says, "Be healed in Jesus' name" until the Kingdom of God is manifested. Our job as fellow believers is to help one another to stand in the righteousness Jesus gives us as a free gift until we receive the blessings God has for us.

God's ways are much higher than our ways and can sometimes be offensive to us. For example, the people of Nazareth were offended by Jesus' humanity and, therefore, He could not do many miracles there because of their unbelief. (see Mark 6:5-6) Religious people were offended by Jesus' approach and, therefore, He would not do any miracles for them to endorse their unbelief. When John the Baptist was uncertain if Jesus was truly the Messiah because His ways were so different than what he expected, Jesus said, "Blessed is the one who is not offended at me." (see Matthew 11:6) If we find ourselves offended by Jesus or His ways of leading us, then we are in unbelief and will find it challenging to receive from Him.

This said, Jesus does not condemn unbelief and God's Kingdom can manifest in spite of unbelief. It only takes a mustard seed of faith for mountains to be moved. Therefore, do not ever condemn yourself or anyone else for struggling with unbelief, and do not make faith into a self-righteous performance-driven way of meeting God's criteria for blessing. Jesus met all of God's requirements for you. Start with the faith that you have in this and cry out to God to help your unbelief!

In Real Life

Prior to my walk with the Lord, I had never been a sickly person with the exception of my chronic skin condition and an allergy to pork. I typically had one flu-like sickness per year, which I had always regarded as a necessary break from my workaholic schedule. I ate a healthy diet and exercised regularly. My only vice was that I enjoyed red wine...probably a little too much.

As I began to walk in total surrender to the Lord, the Holy Spirit directed me to move to a new city, give away everything I owned, and trust God for all of my material needs. Then, the Lord sent me to live in various places with various people. In these places, I engaged my faith in the blood of Jesus and the Lord protected me from lice, colds, flus, and infections. But then, for six months, God sent me to live in one place with a woman who smoked a pack of cigarettes a day in the house and I threw up every day for the first week that I was there. Right after that, I lived in another place in the basement of a house where they had mold issues. Because I had knowledge of the dangers of these environmental factors, I was conscious of the damage they may be doing to my health. Even though I tried to have faith, fear lurked within me.

At the same time, I had little to no control over my diet, had no money for doctors, was under spiritual attack by those who did not believe God had asked me to live by faith, and this was the season in my life when Jesus was teaching me about not defending myself. I did my best to be loving and to turn the other cheek outwardly, but inwardly I was still full of anger, pride, and self-righteousness. Even though I was obeying God's voice and doing what He wanted me to do, I still had some major issues that needed to be put to the cross to die.

My health declined gradually at first and then grew obviously poorer. I was fatigued all the time, had horrible breath, skin issues that took over my whole body, chronic yeast infections, strange dents in my fingernails and toenails, and my stomach and bowels growled loudly and constantly, especially at quiet prayer meetings. In hindsight, I realize that at the lowest point, my body was so toxic I could have died. But at this point, I didn't know what was wrong with me, I was somewhat in denial about my health issues, a little bit in fear, and definitely trying to muscle through it in my own strength.

I wanted to be healed and I believed God could heal me, but I had no idea how God did these things. I was already seeking first the Kingdom of God, meditating on the Word of God day and night, and hearing the Spirit of the Lord loud and clear with God's guidance for me and prophetic words for others. But, God's healing still seemed like a vague and unpredictable thing to me and I settled for accepting the un-Biblical excuses for why God doesn't always heal.

My health continued to decline and I began to pursue God directly for revelation of healing. He faithfully gave it to me. The Holy Spirit also revealed that my condition was a systemic illness, which explained each and every one of my symptoms. I had Candida. In other words, I was full of yeast. Unfortunately, I knew that in the Bible, yeast is a symbol for sin, which meant to me that I was full of sin and its effects. Moreover, yeast is a mold. Biblically speaking this meant that my body, as the house of God and Temple of the Holy Spirit, was full of mold and I knew that the Biblical cure for a moldy house is total destruction. (see Leviticus 14:43-44) Oy vey. This was not good.

Because I was on the full-faith plan with Jesus, I had no alternatives but to trust God to heal me. I had no idea how to go about this but I was far enough along in my walk of faith that I knew it did not include striving and techniques. I was down to bare bones faith and it didn't seem like I had enough to be healed of this disease that had taken over my whole body. I cried out to God, "I believe! Help my unbelief!"

The Holy Spirit showed me that I had to repent of my self-righteousness. Even though I was obeying God faithfully, my faith had shifted to trusting in my own obedience rather than in Jesus' righteousness. This was also evidenced by my mercilessness towards others. Even though I had pretended a few times to proclaim a forgiveness prayer for those who were attacking me and treating me poorly, God knew that it had not been from the heart. The only solution was to take up my cross and die to myself, my pride, and my self-righteousness completely. This time, I finally submitted myself to God's guidance, came into agreement with the Holy Spirit, and returned to believing in Jesus' righteousness rather than my own obedience.

I also fasted at various intervals for a breakthrough of faith for healing. One time, this caused me to vomit in the evening of each day that I fasted. Needless to say, I did not have much to throw up, so it was often more like dry heaving and spitting. But even as I knelt in front of the toilet to be sick, I knew that a spiritual expulsion was taking place. Finally, one day as I was deeply heaving and spitting up, I involuntarily uttered a strange squawk. I instantly knew I had been healed. The sickness or unclean spirit that had been lodged in me had been expelled forever. God had healed me and, in the days and weeks following this, the symptoms of Candida left my life forever. Hallelujah!

There are so many variable factors in this situation that I honestly do not know exactly what it was that brought Candida into my life, how God worked this miracle, or what I did to bring myself into a position of receiving healing. So, please don't go trying to imitate me in this story except for this: Pursue God for your healing. Hold nothing back from Him and obey Him when He speaks, even if it is hard. You believe but perhaps you need God's help with your unbelief. Then, I guarantee that you will see His hand move in your life.

Chapter Ten

THE PRAYER OF FAITH

(FOR OTHERS)

There are no examples of anyone having a "healing ministry" in the New Testament. This said, there are also no examples of any believer who did not have a healing ministry. All of Jesus' disciples were commissioned, authorized, and endued with power to heal the sick, cast out demons, and raise the dead as a demonstration of the Kingdom of God. This applied to the twelve and the seventy-two during Jesus' earthly ministry, to the one hundred and twenty on the day of Pentecost, and to all followers of Jesus throughout the Book of Acts. Jesus Christ is the same yesterday, today, and forever. (see Hebrews 13:8) This means that the same power of God that the early church experienced can be our experience today if we will only believe what they believed and put it into practice.

> *James 5:14-16 - Is* ***anyone among you sick****? Let them* ***call the elders*** *of the church to pray over them and* ***anoint them with oil*** *in the name of the Lord. And the* ***prayer offered in faith will make the sick person well; the Lord will raise them up****. If they have sinned,* ***they will be forgiven****. Therefore confess your sins to each other and* ***pray for each other so that you may be healed.*** *The* ***prayer of a righteous person*** *is powerful and effective.*

In this passage, James starts by saying, *anyone among you*, meaning that healing is readily available. Then, James instructs the sick to seek out elders for prayer. In addition to being someone who holds the position of Elder in the church, this also includes any man or woman who is further along in the faith, regardless of their position in the church and how many years they have been a believer. All believers are encouraged to *pray for one another* because the *prayer of the righteous* has power to produce results. The Good News is that through faith in Jesus, we are all righteous. Therefore, every believer has the ability to pray for one another to be healed and see it happen. Praying the prayer of faith for the sick to be healed involves believing with absolute assurance that they were healed at the cross by the wounds of Jesus, have already received their healing from God, and that their healing will physically manifest as a result of our prayer. When we truly know that God's love for us has established us in righteousness through the sacrifice of Jesus so that sickness has no right to touch us, we will pray for others as if this is also true for them.

The word James used for *prayer* in the phrase *prayer of faith* is not the most commonly used word for prayer but one that means *vow* or *consecration*. Consecrating the sick person to God through faith in Jesus means we are setting them apart in covenant with God. Because the New Covenant was established through the shed blood of Jesus for the forgiveness of our sins, being consecrated into this covenant includes the forgiveness of all sin, redemption from the curse, and deliverance from the all the forces of evil. To make this abundantly clear, James includes *any sins that they have committed will be forgiven*. When we *confess our sins to one another*, we do not do so to merit healing through confession, but rather to openly admit that our faith is not in our own righteousness but entirely in the goodness and mercy of God through the sacrifice and resurrection of Jesus.

To symbolize consecration to God, James instructs us to *anoint the sick with oil*. The oil does not have any power in itself, but is symbolic of the power of the Holy Spirit being at work to quicken their mortal body to life and health. In fact, when James says that *the Lord will raise them up*, he means that they will be roused out of sickness, obscurity, confusion, ruin, and even death. Remember that it was not Lazarus' faith or confession of sin that raised him from the dead, but the power of the prayer of Jesus.

Healing the Sick

As followers of Jesus, we are all authorized to pray for healing, especially for anyone less mature than we are in the faith. This said, Jesus did not send His disciples out to pray for the sick but to ***heal*** the sick the way He did. When Jesus ministered to the sick, He had success with all manner of sickness. We are called to be like Him and walk in the fullness of His anointing. If our ministry to the sick is ineffective in healing them, then we need to allow God to continue to renew our mind, will, and emotions until our ministry manifests the Kingdom of Heaven as if Jesus were the one ministering. This means that every believer on earth will always have room to grow. Since there is no Biblical example of anyone having a healing specialty for one disease over another, if our prayers for healing seem to be more effective in one area over others it is often an indication that we have more faith in that area than in others.

The only place where Jesus was unable to work many miracles aside from healing a few sick people was in His hometown of Nazareth, but this was due to their unbelief. (see Matthew 13:58) However, when Jesus' disciples failed to expel a demon from a boy and asked Jesus why they were unsuccessful, He did not blame the boy's lack of faith but pointed directly and exclusively to the unbelief of His disciples. Jesus had no problem setting the boy totally free from his affliction. Nothing was impossible for Jesus because He loved with God's perfect mercy and put no obstruction in the way of Heaven's power reaching earth. His disciples, however, even though they had already seen countless miracles, healed many sick people, and cast out many demons themselves, still had barriers of unbelief that hindered God's power from flowing freely through them.

> *Matthew 17:20-21 NKJV - So Jesus said to them, "**Because of your unbelief**; for assuredly, I say to you, if you have faith as a mustard seed, you will say to this mountain, 'Move from here to there,' and it will move; and nothing will be impossible for you. "However, **this kind does not go out except by prayer and fasting.**"*

Accordingly, if we minister to the sick and they are not healed, it is imperative that we do not make excuses for ourselves by blaming the sick person for their unbelief and inability to receive healing. In fact, doing so only reveals that we were most likely not ministering to them in the love and mercy of God. Instead, we must take responsibility for the ineffectiveness of our ministry, our own unbelief, or possibly, our lack of obedience to the instructions of the Holy Spirit in the moment. Approaching it this way will keep us humble before God so that we can continue to grow.

More specifically, Jesus taught that this kind of unbelief can only be dealt with through earnest prayer and fasting. We do not fast in order to force God to move on our behalf. We fast in order to move ourselves out of God's way. Voluntarily humbling ourselves before God by willingly abstaining from eating food as our sustenance focuses our attention on Jesus. As we persevere in fasting, the obstructions of the world, the flesh, and the devil are put to death in our hearts so that the voice of the Holy Spirit is magnified and the power and love of God can flow through us without hindrance.

As we begin to trust God and know His love the way Jesus did, we will begin to see results that Jesus did as we minister to others. This said, in order to experience the results that Jesus did, we also have to approach healing the sick in the way He did. Jesus did not doubt God's love or ask God to heal the sick with long-winded prayers of petition. He commanded healing with God's authority because He was confident in God's will for everyone to be free from oppression and sickness.

One aspect of Jesus' approach is that He submitted Himself wholly to God and did only what He saw His Father doing. Practically speaking, this means waiting for and listening to the Holy Spirit to guide us. The Holy Spirit may whisper to us the name of an unclean spirit that is oppressing the sick person so that we can take authority over the spirit and tell it to leave them in the name of Jesus. Or, the Holy Spirit may whisper in our spiritual ears to command their body or body parts to be healed in the name of Jesus. We can obey these promptings by saying something such as, "Spine, be healed, in Jesus name." As we pray, the Holy Spirit may show us a picture in our mind's eye of us laying our hands on their head, shoulder, or in the place of their affliction so that God's power can flow through us. Remember, Jesus sometimes healed by spitting in mud and rubbing it on blind eyes, so we have to be open to whatever we see the Father doing for the person standing in front of us even if it seems weird or undignified. (see John 9:6)

Also, the Holy Spirit does not always lead us in ways that fit our way of thinking. For example, one person may be in a wheelchair and another person may have a simple toothache. It often seems right to our way of thinking that the wheelchair situation needs urgent attention and the toothache can wait, but the Holy Spirit may direct us to heal the toothache and do nothing for the person in the wheelchair. The Holy Spirit's leading is often far more targeted than we expect.

In fact, Jesus did not go around healing every sick person just because they were sick. He healed everyone who came to Him in faith. Practically speaking, this means that we can only pray the prayer of faith according to the faith we have for them and this is often directly related to their faith for healing. For example, a sick person who comes to us in faith, particularly someone who does not yet know Jesus or a new believer whose faith has not yet been polluted with wrong teaching, is very easy to heal and requires only a little effort on our part. This said, when a sick person comes to us for healing, the Holy Spirit may lead us to ask them questions, like the ones Jesus asked people, which are designed to draw out their faith so that they can receive their healing. If unbelief is uncovered instead, we can minster to them to build their faith in the moment, watching and listening for how they respond. If there is not enough faith present for healing to manifest, then as an alternative to commanding healing in the name of Jesus, we can still pray for them by praying for them to receive deeper revelation of healing, or for God to give them an increase of faith. However, if we bulldoze through a healing prayer for someone without spiritually discerning that they have adopted a mindset of believing that God no longer heals or is not going to heal them and then our prayer fails, our failure may only foster their wrong thinking and lead them into more discouragement and unbelief. It is better to wait in awkward silence for God to truly speak and manifest His healing power than to pray an imitation prayer of half-hearted faith for someone who may be stuck in unbelief and unable to receive.

To illustrate this further, in Lystra, the apostle Paul had spiritual discernment that a man in the crowd, who had been crippled since birth, had faith to be healed. So, Paul commanded him to stand and the man was totally cured. (see Acts 14:9) In another example, Paul (who had worked exceptional and remarkable healing miracles by God's power) left his friend Trophimus behind on a missionary journey because Trophimus was ill. For one reason or another, Paul did not heal

Trophimus. (see 2 Timothy 4:20) Also, from the love that Paul expresses for Epaphroditus, Paul's fellow soldier and co-worker in the Lord's work, it is safe to assume that they had some heart-to-heart conversations about not doing service that the Philippians should have been doing but that Epaphroditus insisted on doing it anyway, even to the detriment of his health. If someone will not listen, we cannot force them. Paul credits God's mercy alone for healing him. (see Philippians 2:25-29)

The point is that no matter how the person in front of us is asking us to pray for them, we take our cues from God through the Holy Spirit and not from the demands of people. When Jesus heard that Lazarus was dying, He waited two more days before making His way to heal him. (see John 11:6) We must always remember that, like Jesus, we do not report to pain, to circumstances, or to people but to God.

It is also worth noting that God is not limited by us in any way. God can do what He wants, when He wants, how He wants, to whom He wants, through whom He wants, and at any time that He wants. He is God and He knows what He is doing. One time, King Hezekiah asked for God to heal the people who had set their hearts to seek God even though they had not met the requirements of purification and God honored Hezekiah's prayer. (2 Chronicles 30:17-20) God is sometimes the most glorified through those who seem to be the most unlikely vessels of heaven's power. We are not always going to understand why or how God does what He does or whom He chooses to do it through. The point is that we are not the ones calling the shots—He is. We are His servants to do His work, His way, and at His direction. Our job is to be equipped for every good work and to keep ourselves open to His leading at all times. Moreover, regardless of whether or not supernatural healing is manifested immediately, we must continue to love one another as Jesus has loved us with encouragement to grow and without condemnation.

Persevere Until Healing Manifests

Once we have revelation of healing, we must remain relentless and uncompromising about the fact that it is God's will for the sick to be well. If you have not yet attained results of supernatural healing when you pray for the sick, don't give up. Don't make excuses. Don't blame the sick person's lack of faith. Humbly admit your own failures but don't dwell on them. Press forward for all that Jesus died to give you and to do all the good works that God prepared for you since before the beginning of the earth. (see Ephesians 2:10) For every follower of Jesus, this includes healing the sick, casting out demons, and raising the dead.

If you receive healing prayer from someone who is known, even all over the world, for being used by God to work miracles, healings, signs, wonders, and even raise the dead but you are not healed when they pray for you, then do not accuse them of being a charlatan or snake oil salesman. When the demon-possessed boy's father speculated about Jesus' ability to heal his son, Jesus accepted no blame for any inability by pointing back to the man's own faith. (see Mark 9:23) This said, don't give way to discouragement or the false belief that you are the exception to the rule and it is not God's will to heal you or that you have some kind of spiritual obstruction getting in the way of your healing. Jesus removed every obstruction for us so that we can freely receive our healing from Him. Don't give up. Keep trusting God and pressing on in faith that it is His will for you to be well with or without anyone else praying for you.

Lastly, if you are sick and cannot find someone in your church who is equipped to heal you by praying the prayer of faith, then pray the prayer of faith for yourself. Your body is a created thing and you have authority over it in the name of Jesus. Believe God with Jesus as your only mediator and receive the healing that Jesus freely gives you.

In Real Life

One morning, I was at the gym when the Lord pointed out a bulky, mean-looking, muscle-builder to me and told me that he was suffering demonic oppression. The Lord wanted me to pray for him and set him free. It was only my first week at this gym and I didn't want to lose my gym membership on account of praying for people, so I went about my workout as if God has not spoken to me. After returning home, I carried on with my day but began to have a mild case of regret for not obeying God. The next day, the Lord pointed out the same man to me with the same instructions. This time, I protested in dialog with God and went about my workout as if God had not spoken to me. I mean, seriously...did God expect me to get on the treadmill next to a man who was already upset about life and could clearly demolish me with a flex of his muscles and tell him that he was tormented by demons? As this day proceeded, my case of regret went from mild to moderate. The next day, I went to the gym and did not see the guy. My case of regret became acute. I apologized to God, confessed my disobedience, and told Him that if He really wanted me to heal the man then He would have to bring the man to the gym and set it up for me. I went through my workout and made my way over to the stretching area. I sat down and began stretching with my hands on my toes and my face between my knees. When I looked up, the mean-looking, muscle-builder was sitting on the mat next to me. I shared with him what God had revealed to me and he looked at me with a quizzical look as if to say, "How could you know that?" I asked him if I could pray and lay hands on him and he agreed. I prayed succinctly, commanding the unclean spirits to leave him in the name of Jesus and there was a definitive lift of heaviness in the spiritual atmosphere around him. When I finished praying, he looked up with a huge grin on his face and exclaimed, "Hallelujah!" His countenance was visibly different. Jesus had set him free and I got to keep my gym membership. Praise God!

Another time, I was visiting a place of worship where they had signs posted which made it explicitly clear that ministry by those who were not on their ministry team was strictly forbidden. The Lord pointed out to me a woman who was sitting a few chairs away from me but there were no people sitting in between us. Her Bible was open and had a language in it that I had never seen before, so I knew that English was not her native language. A little later on, the Holy Spirit whispered to me, "Lay your hand on her shoulder," and I knew that it was for healing. I rebutted by saying, "But Lord, the signs clearly forbid me from ministering here. He replied, "I know. Lay your hand on her shoulder." I do my best to honor and obey the God-appointed authorities in all situations, but I have come to deeply know that Jesus is my Lord and King and this means obeying His voice is the most important thing. I accepted in advance that the consequence for the action I was about to take may be a reprimand or expulsion from the place of worship even though this would have made me sad because I was enjoying myself. I inched my way over to her and placed my hand on her shoulder. "Be healed," I said to her shoulder. She never looked at me but stayed intently focused on the teaching. I kept my hand in place a little longer and then felt the power of God rush into her shoulder. As it did so, her shoulder in my hand felt as if she were moving her arm even though she was not, which indicated to me that she was receiving her healing. She began to move her neck and arm so I said, "Finish it Lord," and went back to my seat. Later, she approached me and, in broken English, told me that her shoulder had been locked for two years, restricting her arm's range of motion and preventing her from moving her arm above the height of her shoulder. She showed me that now she had total mobility because God had completely healed her shoulder. We praised God together!

Another time, a woman approached me for healing prayer for a condition called Chiggers, which were little bugs that nested in her skin and caused discolored patches and incessant itchiness. I sensed from the Holy Spirit that this was part of the curse of the Law at work in her life, so I laid my hands on some of the patches of affected skin and declared her to be redeemed from the curse of the Law by the sacrifice of Jesus. I also took authority over the Chiggers, for they are merely bugs, and commanded them to leave her and never come back. In the moment, I did not feel any rush of heat or any other physical confirmation of God's presence in my prayer, so I was uncertain whether or not she had received results. But, as God would have it, I saw her about a month later and she told me that she had been healed immediately following my prayer and has had no further outbreaks since. Praise God!

One day, I visited a group where a woman was severely ill. I do not recall her exact condition, but it was severe enough that she was frail, thin, and lived with some kind of pocket heart pump device. I was fully persuaded that it was God's will for her to be well and was eagerly waiting for the Holy Spirit to prompt me to pray for her. I waited and waited and not only did the prompting to pray not come, I really sensed that the Lord was prompting me not to pray for her healing. This was perplexing to me, but I kept pushing in for guidance from the Holy Spirit, figuring that it must be the evil one trying to persuade me not to pray. I even went so far as to announce to the group that I was listening to God to see if I could pray for her healing. Once I said that, a tsunami of unbelief and misbeliefs came pouring out of the sick woman's mouth. I lovingly rebuked her on a few points to challenge her faith, but she was firmly established in her refusal to believe. Similar to what Jesus experienced with the people of Nazareth, her unbelief quenched the Spirit of the Lord, so I no longer had faith to pray the prayer of faith for her. This said, if I had prayed for her just because she was sick because it seemed like the right thing to do, my prayer would have failed. Plus, this would have only multiplied her anger at God and her belief that God was not going to heal her, especially since she knew that others in the group had received healing from God through my prayers. I do not know how this woman is doing now, if she is still alive, or if she ever broke through to faith and received her healing. But, I do know that God loves her and wants her to be well.

It is also worth noting that I have prayed healing for people who then died the next day. I did not condemn myself or fabricate un-Biblical excuses such as saying, "God answered my prayer because they were healed in heaven." Instead, I acknowledged my need to grow. I am still growing.

Along these lines, while it is always God's will for the sick to be well, He desires even more for all of us to grow to maturity in Christ. Because of this, there are times when other believers come to me for healing or to have demonic oppression expelled, but the Lord prompts me instead to teach them how to receive healing for themselves or how to take authority over their infirmity in the name of Jesus so they can grow in their faith. Depending on where people are in their walk of faith with the Lord, it may be time for them to take steps of faith to receive healing on their own so that they can also be strengthened and eventually help others to receive healing. Only the Holy Spirit knows where people are in their walk of faith and how to lead us to minister to them the way Jesus would if He were in the room. Accordingly, let each of us be equipped to pray the prayer of faith for the sick and be ready to do whatever the Holy Spirit prompts us to do at any moment in time. This way, we will all grow to maturity in Christ and the Kingdom of God will be manifested on earth as it is in heaven.

Chapter Eleven
TESTING GOD

As we set our course to believe God for healing, accusations sometimes rise up that we are *putting God to the test*. These accusations can come into our own thoughts or be spoken through the mouths of others, but either way they are a lie from the evil one attempting to dissuade us from trusting God wholeheartedly. The truth is that there are various ways of *putting God to the test*, including negative testing with the expectation of failure and positive testing for genuineness. In fact, in Biblical Greek, these are entirely different words which English translations are unable to reflect well because they each translate as *test* or *testing*. Accordingly, while we must refrain from negatively testing God, positively testing Him is our reason for living and revealing His Kingdom to the world.

Negative Testing

The devil attempted to negatively test Jesus in the wilderness through temptations which were designed to draw Him into sin and expose Him as only human rather than the Son of the Living God. In one of these tests, the evil one told Jesus that if He was the Son of God, He should throw Himself off of the highest point in Jerusalem because God had promised in the Scriptures to send angels to rescue Him. Jesus responded by quoting the Scripture, "You must not put the Lord your God to the test." (see Luke 4:12) The Scripture Jesus used is a quote from the Book of Deuteronomy where Moses admonished the Israelites to not test God the way they had at Massah. (see Deuteronomy 6:16) In the historical account, shortly after the Israelites had walked through the waters of the Red Sea, they came to a place where there was no water and they were thirsty. They started complaining and demanding that Moses give them water to drink and escalated the conflict by arguing that God must have brought them out of Egypt in order to kill them in the wilderness. They no longer believed God was with them, and they became so angry that they were ready to stone Moses to death. The Lord showed Moses how to cause drinking water to miraculously gush out of a rock and the

Israelites drank. Then, Moses named the place Massah which means *testing* because they had tested God by saying, "Is God with us or not?" (see Exodus 17:1-7) This incident and other examples of the Israelites putting God to the test in a negative way are recounted in Psalm 78 as an example to guard us from making the same mistakes. (see 1 Corinthians 10:11) Even when they had seen God work great miracles on their behalf, they tested Him by the way they did not believe Him, by making demands of Him, and by doubting His ability to do what He promised. They forgot His mighty works, spoke against Him, refused to live by His ways, and turned back on the day of battle. At other times, they flattered God with their mouths, but they did not believe Him in their hearts.

> *Psalm 78:18-22 - They* ***willfully put God to the test*** *by demanding the food they craved. They spoke against God; they said, "Can God really spread a table in the wilderness? True, He struck the rock, and water gushed out, streams flowed abundantly, but can He also give us bread? Can He supply meat for his people?" When the LORD heard them, He was furious; His fire broke out against Jacob, and His wrath rose against Israel,* ***for they did not believe in God or trust in His deliverance****.*

In the devil's temptation of Jesus, the evil one tested Jesus by trying to force Jesus to presumptuously put a demand on God's miracle working power in order to prove Himself and His identity. To paraphrase, the devil said, "If you are the Son of God and trust God so much to protect you, then throw yourself off of a building." (see Luke 4:9-11) But, Jesus trusted God and had nothing to prove. Moreover, Jesus never abused God's power or promises for personal amusement, the advancement of His own will, self-defense, or to make a spectacle of Himself in order to gain fame or followers.

The religious people in Jesus' day were also guilty of *putting God to the test*. Even though they had already seen Him work countless signs and wonders for others, they demanded that He perform miraculous signs to prove Himself. Essentially, they said, "If you are the Messiah, do a miracle to prove it." They were also constantly attempting to trap Jesus in His words or actions in order to expose Him as a fraud. Again, Jesus had nothing to prove and worked no miracles for them. In fact, their unbelief was so firmly rooted in their hearts that Jesus said they would not believe even if He raised the dead.

From all of this we see that we test God in a negative way by not believing Him or trusting Him for our salvation, deliverance, healing, and sustenance. We test God through our unbelief in His ability to fulfill His promises, when we doubt His goodness, or think that He has evil intentions for us even if this is what our circumstances seem to indicate. We test God when we make selfish or presumptuous demands of Him as if He has to do anything to prove Himself to us. We test God when our hearts have become so hard that even if He did heal us we would not still not believe Him. Just as Jesus advised His disciples to do, God does not give to dogs what is holy or throw His pearls before pigs. (see Matthew 7:6) We disqualify ourselves from God's blessings by behaving like dogs or pigs when we put God to the test in a negative way.

This said, when the evil one is trying to convince us that believing God for healing is a bad idea, he skews the meaning of testing God to make it seem like believing God for the healing Jesus paid for us to have is *putting God to the test*. In a very subtle way, the devil attempts to work it into our minds that believing in faith that we were healed by Jesus' stripes is the same thing as recklessly throwing ourselves off of a high building. This is a lie. It is not presumptuous to believe that God is willing and able to heal us and that, in fact, He has healed us through the sacrifice of His Son. To the contrary, this is exactly what God wants us to do.

Positive Testing

Because of Jesus' death and resurrection, heaven on earth is our birthright as children of God. Jesus gave His disciples only one prayer to pray and this prayer includes the phrase, "Your Kingdom come, Your will be done, on earth as it is in heaven." (see Matthew 6:10) When Jesus sent His disciples out to proclaim the Kingdom of Heaven, He sent them out with power and authority to demonstrate on earth what heaven is like. Since, there is no sickness, death, or pain in heaven, this means that health is God's will for us and is a demonstration of His Kingdom. We should be the healthiest people on earth. In view of this, our proper form of worship is to offer ourselves to God wholeheartedly in order to test, prove, and be the proof of His abounding goodness toward us.

> *Romans 12:1-2 - Therefore, I urge you, brothers and sisters, in view of God's mercy, to* ***offer your bodies as a living sacrifice,*** *holy and pleasing to God—this is your true and proper worship. Do not conform to the pattern of this world, but be transformed by the renewing of your mind.* ***Then you will be able to test and approve what God's will is—His good, pleasing and perfect will.***

Interestingly, this verse does not say to offer God our hearts or our souls but our *bodies*. It is easy to say with our mouths that we trust God, but it is entirely different to actually trust Him with our bodies. This is why He sent the Holy Spirit to dwell in our hearts to transform our way of thinking from the world's ways, beliefs, approaches, methods, and wisdom to the simplicity of trusting Jesus for our salvation, deliverance, healing, and sustenance. This said, our minds are renewed not through head knowledge of God but through putting our faith into action. We have to continually take steps of faith to *put God to the test* in a positive way by trusting Him to do what only He can do. In fact, the word for *test and approve* in this verse is the same word we referenced in the chapter about testing our faith for genuineness before taking Communion. Like a jeweler inspecting a diamond to confirm that it is real, we are encouraged to test the genuineness of God's perfect and pleasing will—on earth as it is in heaven.

Therefore, each of us should constantly be putting God to the test in a positive way by genuinely trusting Jesus. According to what we truly believe, we can take steps or leaps of faith as an act of worship and with confident expectation that God is willing and able to fulfill all that He has promised by healing us. When we truly do this, He will always be proven to be faithful. Then, we trust Him more so that we can take even greater steps of faith.

In Real Life

In my own life, I have experienced the dynamic of the various ways people test God and how He leads us to respond as His servants. For example, I spoke to a certain well-esteemed religious leader about God healing the sick. In a ministry setting, this leader responded by saying, "Prove it." At this, a Scripture rose up in my spirit, saying, "No sign will be given you except the sign of Jonah," which is what Jesus said when religious leaders demanded a sign from Him. (see Matthew 12:39) In agreement with this direction from the Lord, I purposefully worked no miracles to prove anything. However, over the course of the next several weeks, without me telling anyone about this, person after person went to this leader with story after story of how the Lord had used me to heal them. In contrast, I spoke in the same way to another leader when a woman with a leg injury limped up to us seeking prayer for healing. The leader I was speaking to gestured toward me and said, "She will do it for you." While I knew I was being tested, there was not a hint of unbelief or religious demand. I laid hands on the woman's leg and she was healed with instant relief. One leader tested negatively and the other leader tested positively. The results speak for themselves.

As for me personally, shortly after the Lord challenged me to renounce medicine, I was struck with a horrible flu complete with body aches and fever. At first, I expected it to pass, but it didn't. Instead, I grew worse and became so weak that I could hardly stand up and fear started to kick in as I realized that people have died from the flu. The evil one tried to convince me that trusting God wholeheartedly for healing was presumption and testing Him. I began to doubt my commitment to being healed by faith and felt guilty for not responding with more faith a few days earlier. But soon, I recognized that fear and guilt were classic tactics of the evil one and something greater than fear arose in me. I decided to fight in faith with all the strength I had, which wasn't much. In the living room, in my pajamas, I started preaching the Gospel to myself. This went on for a good hour or so when suddenly my fever broke, my body stopped aching, and my appetite returned. The flu was gone, and I have never had the flu since. Hallelujah!

Incidentally, many of the things I preached to myself on this day are the teachings that are now contained in this book. Aren't you glad I put God's will to the test?

Chapter Twelve

ALLOWING, TEACHING, & MYSTERIES

God is good. God is love. God is a rewarder of those who seek Him. God does not lie, and He does not change His mind. If He has said something, He will do it. He always keeps His promises. His lovingkindness and mercy never ends. God is righteous in all His ways and kind in everything He does. As if all this is not enough, in the New Covenant God delights to bless us and do good to us. (see 1 John 4:8; Hebrews 11:6; Numbers 23:19; Deuteronomy 7:9; Lamentations 3:22-23; Psalm 145:17; Jeremiah 32:41)

God has an enemy who is the father of lies, never tells the truth, always has evil and wicked intent, and is bent on destruction. The evil one is constantly trying to convince us that God is not good, that Jesus is not Lord, and that we have done something to deserve less than the full experience of God's benefits and blessings as His children or that we have to do something to earn it. In addition, the evil one is extremely subtle, a master at deception, and knows the Word of God. (see John 8:44, 10:10; 1 John 4:3; Galatians 3:1; Genesis 3:1; 2 Corinthians 11:3, 14; Matthew 13:19)

God Allowed It

Sometimes, when people are struggling to receive healing from God, they will say things like, "God allowed it" about their illness. Usually, people who believe this understand that God is good and that God does not put disease on us and they usually attribute sickness to original sin and the fallen state of this world. Then, they spend their time self-inspecting for anything they have done that would cause God to "remove His protection" from their lives, or they accept sickness as God's will and settle for less than what Jesus died to give us in the name of "God's sovereignty." They may also reference the book of Job and the way satan stood before God to propose an evil plan against Job, which God permitted him to carry out. (see Numbers 14:9; Job 2:1-6; Isaiah 5:5) Like most of the enemy's tactics, this whole argument seems to make sense and is based in some truth but, nonetheless, it is a lie that pushes us toward the knowledge of good and evil and away from freely given life and health through faith in Jesus.

We live in a fallen world and disease is a part of it. Since the fall of Adam, we earn or deserve sickness through disobedience. When God redeemed Israel and gave His Law, He revealed that the way to stay in health and live a long life is through obedience to Him. When we violate God's Law, we deserve a penalty which can include sickness. If we had not sinned, we would not have warranted punishment. Righteousness is our protection and the way to remain in health.

So far, the "God allowed it" argument seems to be right. However, the way to pay the penalty for disobedience is through a blood sacrifice of high enough value to reconcile us to God and restore us to righteousness and its benefits, including health. Of course, this is exactly what Jesus came to do for us. His blood perpetually pays for us to remain righteous before God. (see 1 John 1:7) As long as our faith is in this, God never removes His protection from us. Moreover, God put His Spirit in our hearts to lead us in faithfulness to Him so that we can receive all of His blessings if we will simply listen and be led by Him.

Therefore, not only does God ***not*** allow sickness—He has paid the price for us to not be sick. Sickness violates the covenant we have with God through faith in Jesus who redeemed us from the effects of the fall of man and transferred us to the Kingdom of Heaven where sickness is forbidden. Moreover, Jesus gave us authority over every disease, unclean spirit, and over the enemy so that we can forbid sickness in our lives. (see Luke 9:1, 10:19; Matthew 18:18) It is our own wrong understanding of what Jesus has done for us, our unbelief in the benefits that God extends freely to us in the New Covenant, or our determination to do things our own way rather than being led by the Holy Spirit that gives sickness a place in our lives. God does not allow sickness—we allow it through unbelief.

In addition to this, in the days of Job, satan had access to the throne room of God in Heaven. Even though Adam had originally been given direct access to God and authority to rule over all creation, he gave up this right and sold it to the evil one when he disobeyed God and ate from the wrong tree. However, when Jesus died on the cross and shed His blood as atonement for the Heavenly Tabernacle, He cleansed the Most Holy Place in Heaven, which is the throne room of God, and expelled all evil including the evil one. (see Hebrews 8, 9:11-12; Leviticus 16:14; John 12:31; Revelation 12:9) Because of this, now, instead of satan being at God's right hand to bring a constant stream of accusations against the righteous, Jesus sits at God's right hand to perpetually intercede for mercy. (see Hebrews 7:25)

Sadly, this "God allowed it" lie of the enemy is most commonly launched against truly pious and devoted people who want to see the will of God done in their lives. But if it is God's will for them to be sick, then it would be against God's will for them to pray to be healed. If it is true that God allowed sickness as His will for their lives, then it would only be obedient to discontinue every form of treatment for sickness because that would be a contradiction against the will of God. Do you see how subtle the enemy is in distorting our view of God and His good will toward us? Instead, it's time to allow ourselves to be led by the Holy Spirit into the fullness of all that God has made available to us through the blood of His Son.

God is Teaching

When people are struggling to receive healing from God, another thing they will say of their sickness is that, "God is teaching me." They will reference Scriptures about God chastising those He loves and how His discipline is painful when it is happening. They will also often speak about how God is using sickness to test their faithfulness. Again, this seems logical and is based in some truth but it is a lie from the evil one.

Jesus took all of our chastisement and all of our sickness upon Himself so that, through faith in Him, we have been healed by His wounds and have been adopted as beloved sons and daughters of God. (see Isaiah 53:4-5; Ephesians 1:5) Therefore, God treats us as His beloved children and does not use sickness to chastise us. As if it is not enough to say that a loving Father would never inflict sickness on their own son or daughter, Jesus is our example of life as a child of God and as a beloved Son, Jesus was never sick. Because of Jesus' sacrifice, we have the same position before God that Jesus does through our faith in Him. Sickness has no right to touch us.

This said, as a beloved Son, Jesus learned obedience through the things He suffered. (see Hebrews 5:8) As we will discuss more in the next chapter, this suffering does not include sickness. In fact, God said He would chastise His Son through the rods of men. (see 2 Samuel 7:14) Moreover, if we look at the whole context of the letter to the Hebrews, which includes the chapter about God's painful discipline for His children, we see that it was written to encourage believers who were suffering severe and ongoing persecution against them for their Christian faith. These are the types of sufferings that Jesus suffered as a Son of God. He remained faithfully and fully persuaded about God's goodness and ability to fulfill His promises and He learned obedience to the will of God through the power of the indwelling Holy Spirit by not giving way to disobedience through sin or the fear of man, even in the face of death. (see Philippians 2:8) As God's sons and daughters, we learn the same kind of obedience when we suffer persecution for the name of Jesus until we are fully mature in the faith and living our lives trusting God the way that Jesus did, unshakable in knowing that we are the righteousness of God. (see Hebrews 5:13-14; 2 Corinthians 5:21) Of course, when we know that we are the righteousness of God, we also know that sickness has no place in the lives of the righteous.

Not only does God ***not*** chastise us through sickness—He laid all sickness upon Jesus so that we can be healed. God does not teach us about His goodness by being evil. God does not teach us about His faithfulness by being fickle. God does not teach us about His love and mercy by attacking our bodies with disease and torment. Moreover, God has given us a teacher and it is not sickness—it is the Holy Spirit. If God is teaching us anything during the course of our sickness, He is teaching us that it is not His will for us to be sick.

Also, James made it clear that we should not say that God is testing us. (see James 1:13-14) God does not test us, sin and the evil one test us. Sin lurks within us, has no regard for God, and is longing for quick solutions, comfort, and personal satisfaction. The evil one is constantly, endlessly, and relentlessly throwing tests and temptations at us, extending offers of instant relief or advancement that usually seem to be a much easier or faster way of achieving the results that we desire than trusting God will produce. Meanwhile, the Holy Spirit is constantly teaching us, leading us in truth, guiding us in paths of righteousness for the Lord's glory, and reminding us of everything that Jesus taught. (see John 14:26) We have to allow the Holy Spirit to renew our mind, will, and emotions so that we come fully into alignment with God's good will toward us in Jesus. As we submit ourselves to God and resist the attacks of the enemy, the evil one will flee from us and so will sickness.

Accordingly, if sickness, doubt, or unbelief is a test that the evil one has thrown into your life, then pass the test by believing deep in your heart that healing from all pain, disease, torment, affliction, and infirmity was included in the New Covenant through the shed blood of Jesus, and by obeying the promptings of the Holy Spirit, who will guide you into health. Until we believe this to the depths of our being and live as sons and daughters of God who are led by His Spirit, we will continue to permit sickness in our lives. If we persist in thinking that "God is teaching us," through sickness, we will allow ourselves to be diverted by learning techniques, methods, and teachings which are birthed out of the knowledge of good and evil rather than righteousness as a free gift from God and healing by Jesus' wounds. We may even acquire lots of knowledge about God and still be sick because we never learn or do not believe that it is God's will for us to be well. (see 2 Timothy 3:5, 7; Colossians 2:23) The enemy will do everything he can to divert us in this way for as long as he is able or until we are too weary to press on in the fight of faith.

It's a Mystery

Another thing people sometimes say when they are struggling to receive healing from God is, "God works in mysterious ways," or "It's a mystery." Usually, this is an indication that they are avoiding repentance from the wrong beliefs that are keeping them sick or that the enemy has worn them out to the point of fatigue in their faith.

God does not work in mysterious ways—He works according to His Word. Moreover, God has not locked up His Kingdom and blessings in secrecy and guesswork. We are God's children, and He desires to open all the storehouses of heaven to us if we will continue to pursue Him for all that He has for us. In fact, Jesus calls us His friends because He tells us everything that the Father has told Him and He opens up all of the secrets of the Kingdom of Heaven to us. (see John 15:15; Matthew 13:11) Not to mention that He sent the Holy Spirit into our hearts to guide us into all truth—not just a little bit of the truth, but all the truth. (see John 16:13) This is why we are encouraged to keep on asking, seeking, and knocking so that we can continue to receive, find, and have more and more of God's goodness opened to us. (see Matthew 7:7-8)

When we do this, we discover that God has revealed the biggest mystery of all redemptive history to us so that we can steward the mystery to the rest of the world. The mystery is this: Jesus Christ was born as God in the flesh who came, died, was raised to everlasting life, ascended to heaven, and poured out His Spirit into our hearts so that we can be just like Him while we are still here on earth. (see Romans 16:25-26; 1 Corinthians 2:7, 4:1; Ephesians 3:4-5; Colossians 1:26-27, 2:2; 1 Timothy 3:16) Nobody was able to be righteous before God, so God had to make a way to put Himself inside us in order for us to have right standing with Him, be blessed, and bring the Kingdom of Heaven to earth until Jesus returns. The mystery was hidden in ages past, but now it is out in the open! Hallelujah!

As we grow with God as His children, we will be constantly marveling in amazement with childlike wonder because we do not always know how He does what He does or why He is so kind, generous, and loving toward us. But, we cannot use God's "mysteriousness" as an excuse for not receiving something from Him that Jesus died to give us. The mystery of God has been revealed and the things that God has revealed have been revealed so that we may do them. (see Deuteronomy 29:29)

Chapter Thirteen

SUFFERING & TRIBULATION

We are not perfected or sanctified through sickness or suffering. We are sanctified by the blood of Jesus, His Word, His name, and by the Holy Spirit. (see Hebrews 10:10, 14; John 15:3, 17:17; 1 Corinthians 6:11; Titus 3:5) Accordingly, because we are sanctified and righteous before God as His sons and daughters, we should be the healthiest people on earth as proof of God's goodness and the evidence of His Kingdom. Unfortunately, one of the lies that the enemy uses to keep believers sick is to convince us that sickness is sharing in the sufferings of Christ or experiencing the tribulations of this world. This is a lie that can cause us to embrace sickness rather than healing as the normal Christian experience.

As we touched on in the last chapter, sharing in the sufferings of Christ does not include sickness. Jesus was never sick. He suffered by giving up the splendors and privileges of heaven in order to be born into a flesh like ours and live completely dependent on God's provision. He suffered when He willingly offered Himself to uncompromisingly obey the will of God, even though it included rejection by His own people and by the world, having insults hurled at Him without retaliating, being led like a lamb to slaughter without defending Himself, and being whipped, scourged, beaten, mocked, betrayed, and ultimately crucified to death while praying for his crucifiers to be forgiven. (see Isaiah 53:3, 7; John 1:11; 1 Peter 2:23-24) Through all of this, Jesus relentlessly trusted in God's goodness and power to bring His promises to pass and unwaveringly prioritized eternal matters over the things of this world. He also demonstrated that sons and daughters of God learn obedience through the things we suffer at the hands of men as we learn to trust steadfastly in God alone and prove Him faithful. Even so, what works to draw us to maturity in Christlikeness is our perseverance in the faith and not the suffering itself. (see James 1:4; Romans 5:3-5)

It is true that Jesus said, "In this world you will have tribulation," and that the apostle Paul said, "It is through many tribulations that we enter the Kingdom of God." (see John 16:33; Acts 14:22) Actually, Paul deeply desired to share in the sufferings of Christ and there are many passages throughout the New Testament about suffering for the Christian faith. (see Philippians 3:10; Romans 8:17; 2 Timothy 3:12) But none of these include sickness. In fact, the word used for *tribulation* means *pressing or pressure, trouble, oppression, distress, the afflictions of those hard pressed by siege and the calamities of war and the straights of want*. The words used to describe *sharing in the sufferings* of Christ are defined as *an external suffering, hardship, or pain* ***of the same kind***, or *to suffer evils, particularly persecutions,* ***in like manner***. We follow a crucified King. When we live our lives for the Kingdom of God by following Jesus and doing the things that He did, we wage war against the kingdom of the evil one. It is a clash of kingdoms that the world takes note of and that is opposed by all the forces of darkness. In fact, when Jesus was with His disciples and teaching them to remain faithful to Him, the very next thing He taught was that the world will hate us as His followers. (see John 15; Matthew 24:9) Jesus also taught in His parable of the soils that persecution and tribulation reveal how deeply committed we are in our faith and if His word has truly taken root in our hearts. And yet, none of the soils in this parable include sickness. (see Matthew 13:20-21) Moreover, when Jesus' first disciples suffered persecution for the faith, it was largely due to the fact that they were healing the sick in Jesus' name. For this, they rejoiced to be counted worthy to suffer. (see Acts 5:29)

To demonstrate this further, the Apostle Peter's first letter was written for the purpose of encouraging believers to endure through persecution from the world. Such sufferings prove the genuineness of our faith and establish us even more firmly in Christ. (see 1 Peter 1:7, 5:7-10) In this letter, Peter emphasizes that suffering for doing the right thing and obeying God may indeed be God's will for us but this is different than suffering for doing wrong. As such, all suffering is suffering, but not all suffering is suffering for righteousness' sake. (see 1 Peter 3:13-17) For example, losing your job may be a form of suffering but it is only suffering for righteousness' sake if you were fired due to your Christian faith. However, if you were fired for your own errors, then your suffering is from your own sin. This said, even if we suffer for our own faults and failures, God is so gracious and faithful that He works everything out for our good. (see Romans 8:28) Nevertheless, there is a clear distinction between generalized suffering and suffering for the faith. It is in this same letter that Peter points to Jesus as our example to follow when we suffer and firmly attests that we were healed of our diseases by His wounds. (see 1 Peter 2:19-24)

Similarly, the letter to the Hebrews was also written to encourage Jewish followers of Jesus who were growing weary due to ongoing and brutal persecution, which had lasted longer and been fiercer than they had originally anticipated. When they first came to faith, they had been disowned by their families as if they were dead, were publicly ridiculed, beaten, imprisoned, and robbed of everything they owned due to their faith in Jesus as their Messiah, and they had joyously endured all of this. (see Hebrews 10:32-34) But, these attacks against them continued relentlessly for many years and they were encouraged to follow the example of faithful believers from the past who are listed by name in Hebrews Chapter 11. None of the trials endured by these heroes of the faith included sickness but pertained to obeying God at the expense of the things of this world and in spite of the hatred of men. During their lifetimes, God faithfully fulfilled many promises to them. The promise that they died without receiving was to see God ruling and reigning on the earth as their King. They lived their lives faithfully waiting for this, considering themselves to be citizens of heaven even while they were foreigners and nomads on the earth.

These types of sufferings are the chastisement of God to His sons and daughters, which proves our legitimacy as His children and brings us to a place of total peace and trust in our heavenly Father. (see Hebrews 12:5-11) These types of trials cause us to stop trusting in our own strength and to grow in our understanding that we are established in righteousness through our faith in Christ. (see Hebrews 5:13) Of course, this includes the fact that since health is a condition of righteousness, then sickness is not suffering for righteousness sake.

On a different note, while Jesus was on the cross, He bore all of our sicknesses in totality as the one and only Savior, Deliverer, and Healer.

This means that even though we are called to be like Jesus in every possible way, we do not bear the sickness of others. Praying to God to have someone's sickness imputed to us, even in part, or thinking that we can somehow "carry the burden" of another person through sickness the way that Jesus did for us may sound like a good Christian thing to pray or do but, unfortunately, it is a lie from the pit of hell and a trap of the evil one. If we have enough faith to believe that God can move sickness around so readily, then we should just learn to pray the prayer of faith for healing and make the sick person well.

I am not saying that sickness is not suffering—it is. Since the fall of Adam, there have been many and various forms of suffering in this world, including sickness. However, when we read Scriptures about glorying or being patient in tribulation, rejoicing in suffering, or receiving the Lord's comfort in our trials, we should know that sickness and disease are not what is being addressed. (see Romans 5:3, 12:12; Colossians 1:24; 2 Corinthians 1:4) Jesus did not comfort the sick in their sickness, ask them to be patient, or perpetuate their sickness in any way—He healed the sick. Therefore, healing and health are what Jesus demonstrated to be God's will for us and what He has made available to us when we place our faith in Him. While it is true that we are exhorted to rejoice always in all things, including suffering and sickness, we should not embrace or glory in our sickness as the Lord's will for us when Jesus died on a cross to pay for our healing.

Chapter Fourteen
A THORN IN THE FLESH

Another strategy of deception the evil one has used to keep believers in bondage to sickness is to convince us that we will not be healed because our illness is a *thorn in the flesh,* similar to the one the Apostle Paul had. However, when we look at any given Scripture we must take it in view of the context in which it was delivered. This includes understanding the writer, the audience to whom they are speaking, the purpose of their writing, the words they use, and other aspects which can help to give us accurate insight. Accordingly, when we understand what Paul was referring to as his *thorn in the flesh*, we will see rather quickly that it is highly improbable that the thorn refers to lingering illness or that the average believer warrants such a thorn, leaving us with no excuse for settling for receiving less than the healing Jesus died to give us.

This is what the Apostle Paul said about his *thorn in the flesh*:

> *2 Corinthians 12:6-10 - Even if I should choose to boast, I would not be a fool, because I would be speaking the truth. But I refrain, so no one will think more of me than is warranted by what I do or say, or because of these surpassingly great revelations. Therefore, in order to keep me from becoming conceited,* ***I was given a thorn in my flesh, a messenger of Satan, to torment me****. Three times I pleaded with the Lord to take it away from me. But He said to me, "My grace is sufficient for you, for My power is made perfect in weakness." Therefore I will boast all the more gladly about my weaknesses, so that Christ's power may rest on me. That is why, for Christ's sake, I delight in weaknesses, in insults, in hardships, in persecutions, in difficulties. For when I am weak, then I am strong.*

A Scriptural Figure of Speech

Paul was a Jewish man and, before becoming a follower of Jesus, he was schooled in the Scriptures with the finest education in the world in his day and was known to have excelled in his studies because of his extreme zealousness for God and His Word. (see Galatians 1:14) In light of this, in several of Paul's letters, he used figures of speech from the Scriptures that were commonly known among his people. For example, in Paul's letter to Timothy, he said that the Lord had *saved him from the lion's mouth.* (see 2 Timothy 4:17) In this, Paul was not referring to a literal lion. Being thrown to literal lions did eventually become a form of torturous persecution against Christians but that had not yet begun when Paul was writing this letter to Timothy. This said, in Jewish history there was a man who was literally delivered from the lion's mouth by God—Daniel. (see Daniel 6; Hebrews 11:33) Hence, Paul was using an expression common to the Jewish people as a means of saying that even though no human had come to his defense, the Lord had spared him from enemies seeking to destroy him.

It was in this same manner that Paul used the expression *thorn in the flesh.* Paul did not mean that he had a literal thorn in his flesh but was using a figure of speech from the Scriptures. In the history of Israel, the Lord instructed the Israelites to destroy and drive out all the inhabitants who were occupying the Promised Land. He warned them that the inhabitants from the other nations would become like *thorns in the flesh* if the Israelites failed to drive them out completely because the wrong beliefs and practices of the nations would steer the Israelites away from worshiping Him as the only true God. Moses was the first one to use this expression, and it was also used by Joshua, the prophet Ezekiel, and the author of the Book of Judges.

> *Numbers 33:52, 55 - ...**Drive out all the inhabitants of the land before you**. Destroy all their carved images and their cast idols, and demolish all their high places. ... But if you do not drive out the inhabitants of the land, **those you allow to remain will become barbs in your eyes and thorns in your sides**. They will give you trouble in the land where you will live.*
>
> *Joshua 23:13 - ...then you may be sure that the LORD your God will no longer **drive out these nations before you**. Instead, **they will become snares and traps for you, whips on your backs and thorns in your eyes**, until you perish from this good land, which*

the LORD your God has given you.

Judges 2:3 ESV - "So now I say, I will not drive them out before you, but ***they shall become thorns in your sides****, and their gods shall be a snare to you."*

Ezekiel 28:24 - No longer will the people of Israel have ***malicious neighbors who are painful briers and sharp thorns****. Then they will know that I am the Sovereign LORD.*

In other places, including in the New Testament, thorns are used as a figure of speech for people who have departed from uprightness, stir up division, and are unable to produce good spiritual fruit. For example:

Micah 7:2-4a - The faithful have been swept from the land; not one upright person remains. Everyone lies in wait to shed blood; they hunt each other with nets. Both hands are skilled in doing evil; the ruler demands gifts, the judge accepts bribes, the powerful dictate what they desire-- they all conspire together. ***The best of them is like a brier, the most upright worse than a thorn hedge****.*

Hebrews 6:8 - But land that ***produces thorns and thistles*** *is worthless and is in danger of being cursed. In the end it will be burned. (Referring to believers who fall away from the faith.)*

Mark 4:18-19 - Still others, ***like seed sown among thorns****, hear the word; but the worries of this life, the deceitfulness of wealth and the desires for other things come in and choke the word,* ***making it unfruitful****.*

Poignantly, when the rulers of this world crucified the King of all the earth, they mocked Him and His authority by placing a crown of thorns on His head.

Matthew 27:29 - ...And then twisted together ***a crown of thorns*** *and set it on his head. They put a staff in his right hand. Then they knelt in front of him and mocked him. "Hail, king of the Jews!" they said.*

When Paul wrote about his *thorn in the flesh*, it was in a letter to the believers in Corinth in response to the fact that false apostles were attacking Paul and mocking his apostolic authority. These false apostles took advantage of the Corinthian believers in order to strengthen themselves, gain a following, make a profit, or become famous teachers of the Scriptures. Paul on the other hand, defended his ministry and apostleship by boasting in the way he shared in the weakness and sufferings of Christ for the Kingdom of God. While this boasting seemed like foolishness to Paul, he thought it was necessary in order to combat the errors in the Corinthian's view of the Christian life and the arguments of his accusers.

Paul described his thorn as *a messenger of satan sent to torment him*. The word he used for *messenger* is most commonly used to describe the angels of God but, in this case, Paul uses it to describe a messenger from satan. In the same way that God's angels work things out for the good of God's children, satan's messengers stir up malice, murder, and deception against them. This word is never used to describe a spiritual condition in a person's body, and it is not the same word used to describe the demons that oppress people with infirmity. Additionally, the word *torment* is more accurately translated as *buffet* because the word literally means *to strike with the fist, to maltreat, and to treat with violence.* While sickness in our bodies can metaphorically feel like this, the experiences Paul used to describe his thorn leaves little room for an internal, allegorical, or spiritualized interpretation of what he meant about being attacked. Here is part of how Paul described the buffetings of his *thorn in the flesh*:

> *2 Corinthians 11:23-28 - Are they servants of Christ? (I am out of my mind to talk like this.) I am more. I have* ***worked much harder****,* ***been in prison more frequently****, been* ***flogged*** *more severely, and been* ***exposed to death*** *again and again. Five times I received from the Jews the* ***forty lashes*** *minus one. Three times I was* ***beaten with rods****, once I was* ***pelted with stones****, three times I was* ***shipwrecked****, I spent a night and a day in the open sea, I have been constantly on the move. I have been* ***in danger from rivers, in danger from bandits, in danger from my fellow Jews, in danger from Gentiles; in danger in the city, in danger in the country, in danger at sea; and in danger from false believers****. I have labored and toiled and have often gone* ***without***

> ***sleep****; I have known* ***hunger and thirst and have often gone without food****; I have been* ***cold and naked****. Besides everything else, I face daily* ***the pressure of my concern for all the churches****.*

Paul was literally, brutally, repeatedly, and physically assaulted by people in this world who refused to believe Jesus and by worldly believers who rejected his God-given authority. His boasting in these persecutions immediately precedes and follows his use of the expression *thorn in the flesh.* Accordingly, it seems fairly clear to me that persecution is what Paul was referring to as his *thorn in the flesh.* For someone to claim that Paul's thorn is some kind of illness or disease seems like a drastic leap out of the context of his letter to the Corinthians and the whole of Scripture. Also, since many claim that Paul's *thorn in the flesh* was a problem with his eyes or point to the bodily illness that first brought Paul to the Galatians, it is worth noting that Paul arrived in Galatia after being stoned by the crowd at Lystra so inhumanely that they thought he was dead. (see Galatians 4:13; Acts 14:19) It would not be surprising if his body and his eyes were in a weakened or infirm state after such treatment. Moreover, this is the same time and place that Paul encouraged believers and new converts to the faith by saying, "We must go through many tribulations to enter the Kingdom of God." (see Acts 14:22)

The Purpose of the Thorn

But let's not stop there. We may still be left with the question of why God would allow *thorns in the flesh* in the first place, especially for His chosen people and the most influential apostle the world has ever known. Fortunately, God is so good that He states His purposes clearly. The nations that the Israelites were unable to drive out were left there by God in order to test the Israelites in their faithfulness to Him as the one true God and to teach them His methods for fighting battles.

> *Judges 3:1-4 - These are the nations* ***the LORD left to test all those Israelites*** *who had not experienced any of the wars in Canaan (****he did this only to teach warfare*** *to the descendants of the Israelites who had not had previous battle experience): the*

> *five rulers of the Philistines, all the Canaanites, the Sidonians, and the Hivites living in the Lebanon mountains from Mount Baal Hermon to Lebo Hamath.* ***They were left to test the Israelites to see whether they would obey the LORD's commands****, which he had given their ancestors through Moses.*

The Scriptural pattern reveals that unbelievers and false prophets test believers' devotion to the truth and God uses these types of trials to train us in the way of righteousness. (see Deuteronomy 13:1-11; Matthew 13:28-30; 2 Thessalonians 2:11; Hebrews 5:8)

In addition to this, Paul clearly articulated his understanding of why he was given a *thorn in the flesh.* It is also worth noting that Paul is the only person recorded in Scripture to have a *thorn in the flesh.*

> *2 Corinthians 12:7 KJV - And* ***lest I should be exalted above measure*** *through the abundance of the revelations, there was given to me a thorn in the flesh, the messenger of Satan to buffet me,* ***lest I should be exalted above measure****.*

Paul singlehandedly had greater and deeper revelation knowledge of the Scriptures than anyone else on the earth in his day. In the passage leading up to speaking about his *thorn in the flesh*, Paul spoke about the visions, revelations, and out-of-body spiritual experiences of being caught up in paradise that the Lord had given him. Even the other apostles who had walked with Jesus had difficulty understanding the weightiness of Paul's teaching at times. (see 2 Peter 3:16) Through Paul's preaching to the unsaved, great multitudes of unbelievers converted to the Christian faith. He and his apostolic teams established most of the churches in the world in his time, and he trained many of the people who evangelized in other places. Paul also moved in so much of God's miracle power that countless numbers of people were healed of diseases and delivered from demonic oppression through his ministry. Even those who touched cloths he had touched were healed. (see Acts 19:11) Paul walked in so much Kingdom power and preached the Gospel so boldly that, in some cities, people bowed down to him and began to worship him as if he were a god. (see Acts 14:11-12) He had so much apostolic authority in the Church that people wanted to be known as followers of Paul rather than followers of Jesus. (see 1 Corinthians 1:12, 3:4)

According to Paul, he was given a *thorn in the flesh* so that no one, including himself, would exalt him above his rightful status as a servant of the exalted One, Jesus. Persecution from unbelievers and false prophets keeps us humble by keeping us dependent on God for strategies of spiritual warfare.

> *2 Corinthians 1:9 - Indeed, we felt we had received the sentence of death. But this happened* ***that we might not rely on ourselves but on God****, who raises the dead.*

Persecution from unbelievers and false prophets also has a way of preventing others from overly exalting us because false accusations lead to speculations, which cause others to doubt our position in the Kingdom of God. This is exactly what was happening among the Corinthians, some of whom were being swayed away from Paul's apostolic authority, and it was also the case when everyone abandoned Jesus when He was accused of working for the devil and put on trial as a blasphemer.

We must never forget that we follow a crucified King who calls upon us to take up our own cross and follow after Him in these types of sufferings. (see Luke 9:23) God is not going to take away the cross that Jesus told us to carry. When we look at Paul's thorn in this way, it makes perfect sense that God refused to take the thorn away and that Paul learned to delight in it. Suffering for the name of Jesus and for the Kingdom of God due to persecution is cause for great rejoicing. (see Matthew 5:10-13)

Power Made Perfect in Weakness

God left His people, Israel, surrounded by enemy nations which became *thorns in their flesh* so that His power of defending and sustaining them would be revealed through their continued existence and prosperity, in spite of their small stature and little strength compared to other nations. The Apostle Paul suffered constant persecution as his *thorn in the flesh* for essentially the same reason.

In the passage about Paul's thorn, he said that he delighted in weakness, insults, hardships, and persecutions because God's power is made perfect in weakness. This is the same kind of weakness that Jesus entered into by being born in a powerless flesh like ours, tested in all points by the evil one, and crucified on a cross unto death even though He could have called the whole thing off to save His own life. Jesus was never sick and He did not die from sickness. But, through voluntary weakness, He suffered at the hands of wicked men and was then raised from the dead by the power of God. Following the same pattern, even though Paul was a highly competent and capable person, he willingly submitted himself to weakness so that even in the face of insults, hardship, and persecutions, it was exceedingly obvious that Paul's power was not his own, but God's. Jesus and Paul both chose a lifestyle of dependence on God and not their own strength. Paul did not say, "When I am weak, then God is strong" because God is strong all the time. Paul said, "When I am weak, then I am strong" because through voluntary powerlessness, God's power is put into full effect. The Apostle Peter also encouraged believers in this experience.

> *1 Peter 4:14 - If you are insulted because of the name of Christ, you are blessed,* ***for the Spirit of glory and of God rests on you****.*

Paul only wanted to be known for the work God had done through him both in word and deed. He refrained from going into great detail about the surpassing greatness of his revelations, and he cautioned believers about those who go on too extensively about their visions because it results in false humility and disconnection from Christ. (Colossians 2:18) Instead of boasting in his natural and spiritual strengths, Paul chose to boast in his weaknesses so that the power of Christ would rest upon him. On that note, the power of the Holy Spirit *coming upon* or *resting upon* us is always used in the context of supernaturally strengthening us to stand in faith for the truth of the Gospel and to serve other people—including power for healing them! For example:

> *Luke 4:18 KJV -* ***The Spirit of the Lord [is] upon me****, because he hath* ***anointed me to preach*** *the gospel to the poor; he hath* ***sent me to heal*** *the brokenhearted, to* ***preach deliverance*** *to the captives, and recovering of* ***sight to the blind****, to* ***set at liberty them that are bruised****...*

> *Acts 1:8 - "But* ***you will receive power when the Holy Spirit comes on you****; and you will be my witnesses in Jerusalem, and in all Judea and Samaria, and to the ends of the earth."*

In fairness, the word Paul uses for *weakness* can be and is translated as *infirmity* in other places. This said, in every place where it is used to describe infirmity in the form of sickness or disease, it refers to an infirmity that Jesus healed or took upon Himself on the cross. However, more frequently it is used to describe the general condition of human weakness in the context of suffering, calamity, lack of power for speech or understanding, and the sufferings of Christ. Additionally, *weakness* is only one of four words which Paul used to describe the sufferings his thorn caused him to experience—the others being *insults, hardships, and persecutions* which do not include illness.

This said, it is true that when we are sick, we become needy and more dependent on the Lord than normal. Because of this, we can often experience His presence with us in our time of need. The Holy Spirit dwelling within us may speak words of comfort to us, give strength to our mortal bodies to help us do what we cannot do ourselves, and we may also experience the Holy Spirit coming upon us as we minister to others when we are in a weakened state because of illness. However, even if we experience the power of Christ resting upon us because we are in a weakened state due to illness, this does not mean that sickness is a *thorn in the flesh,* so we should not embrace it as one. If we are delighting in sickness because we experience more of God's presence or power in ministry, or if we are choosing to embrace sickness as God's will rather than believing that Jesus paid for it in full at the cross, then we have become ensnared by the lies of the evil one. It is impossible to delight in sickness and in Christ our Healer at the same time. Moreover, it should not take involuntary illness for us to maintain a humble state of dependence on the Lord when we can voluntarily submit ourselves to weakness in addition to receiving our healing that Jesus paid for at the cross.

Lastly, it does not make logical sense for Paul's thorn to be a sickness due to the fact that the Lord spoke of His power being made perfect in weakness. To *make perfect* means to *carry through to completion.* What Jesus clearly revealed through His perfect application of God's will and power is that the completed work of God's power toward sickness is healing! Therefore, if Paul's thorn or weakness was some form of sickness, then Christ's power being made perfect would have healed him.

Blessed

Jesus never said *blessed are the sick*—He healed the sick. But, Jesus decreed a double portion blessing with cause for rejoicing to those who are persecuted for the Kingdom of God.

> *Matthew 5:10-12 - "**Blessed are those who are persecuted** because of righteousness, for theirs is the kingdom of heaven. **Blessed are you when people insult you, persecute you and falsely say all kinds of evil against you because of Me**. Rejoice and be glad, because great is your reward in heaven, for in the same way they persecuted the prophets who were before you."*

Undoubtedly, Paul's *thorn in the flesh* caused him great difficulty and frustration in his pursuit of proclaiming the Gospel to the ends of the earth. However, every time this messenger of satan buffeted him, he knew that great rewards were being accumulated for him in heaven. Hence, his thorn became cause for great rejoicing.

To some degree or another, every believer who desires to live a godly life for Christ will experience persecution for our faith. (see 2 Timothy 3:12) However, without revelation and Kingdom power experiences that resemble the Apostle Paul's, it is highly doubtful that the average believer is deserving of an irremovable *thorn in the flesh* to keep us from becoming conceited. Therefore, for us to claim that we have a *thorn in the flesh* like Paul's or that our illness is our *thorn in the flesh* is an arrogant self-deception. Either we think we are someone when we are not, or we have given way to self-pity rather than contending in faith for our healing. This is not the kind of conceit that warrants a thorn. Instead, we need to learn to humble ourselves before God, submit ourselves to Him, and receive from Him the healing that Jesus died to freely give us.

Chapter Fifteen
MEDICINE & REMEDIES

Once we have experienced the healing power of God, it is hard to settle for anything less. God's methods have no negative side effects, no life-shortening ramifications, repair our bodies to original condition or better, and it's ours as a free gift! However, it has been said that everyone wants a miracle, but nobody wants to need a miracle. As I said in the Introduction to this book, when our health is on the line, what we truly believe about God and what Jesus has done for us is exposed. Oftentimes, when it comes to our health, instead of admitting that we are afraid for our lives and don't actually trust God to heal us, we take control of the situation in the name of "stewardship of our bodies" rather than offering our bodies to God to prove His perfect will. This is why sometimes it is only when we have exhausted all other methods and cry out for God's help in unfeigned sincerity that He steps in and heals us instantly. If we want to be cured by trusting in physicians, medicine, remedies, diet, and exercise, God will let us pursue these other methods to our heart's content. But it is a deception to believe that pursuing other methods is the same as pursuing God as our Physician and Healer. When Jesus said it only takes a mustard seed of faith, He did not mean faith in Him plus any other solution. And when it comes to truly miraculous healings by His supernatural intervention, God does not share His glory with anyone or anything.

When God promised to be the Israelites' Healer, He promised to be their Physician. The Hebrew word for *physician* is *rapha*, which also means to *heal, mend, or cure*. Interestingly, the passage of Isaiah 53, which we have used so much throughout this book about God's healing, also uses this word to describe how we were healed by the stripes of Jesus.

> *Exodus 15:26 - He said, "If you listen carefully to the LORD your God and do what is right in His eyes, if you pay attention to His commands and keep all His decrees, I will not bring on you any of the diseases I brought on the Egyptians, for I am the*

*LORD, **who heals you**." [Rapha – your Physician.]*

*Isaiah 53:5 - But He was pierced for our transgressions, He was crushed for our iniquities; the punishment that brought us peace was on Him, and by His wounds we are **healed**. [Rapha – cured by God, our Physician.]*

Technically speaking, this means that by the wounds of Jesus, we have already been treated by the Great Physician—God. Our job is simply to believe this is true. This is not a matter of denying that there are other methods available to us to cure our illnesses, infirmities, and infections. This is a matter of seeking God in order to know Him as our Healer and experience His healing power in our lives, to the neglect of other methods.

It is often said that, "God uses doctors." Yes, He can. God can work in all things and through all things however He likes. But when King Asa of Judah consulted with physicians without consulting with God, God was not pleased and Asa died. (see 2 Chronicles 16:12-13) This is tragic, particularly because Asa had been a faithful King for most of his reign. However, immediately prior to his illness, Asa had been rebuked by Hanani the seer for making an alliance with the king of Aram rather than trusting God to give him the victory in battle. In essence, by turning to physicians, Asa had done the same thing in the battle for his health. He did not seek the Lord's help but instead sought the aid of men.

Please hear me. I am not against physicians, and I believe that we can be on the same team, pulling for the same goal. However, the more we truly believe God when He says He is our Physician, the more a human substitute becomes less and less appealing. Human physicians can diagnose what is wrong with us and offer repairs or remedies to keep us in decent working condition, but they cannot heal the way God heals. They are often the ones who are the most confounded when someone they thought was beyond assistance comes in miraculously healed by the power of God. Regardless of this, the real issue at hand is not the physicians themselves but what we are placing our trust in for our healing. Cursed is the man who trusts in man and blessed is the man who trusts in God. (see Jeremiah 17:5, 7) This is not limited to physicians but applies when we put our faith in the counsel, knowledge, or strength of any person other than Jesus.

It is often noted that Luke, who wrote the Book of Luke and the Book of Acts, was a physician. However, there is no evidence that he used his medical training to cure anyone while traveling with Paul on missionary journeys or after coming to faith in Jesus. Instead, there is much evidence that he used his intelligence and research skills to write an accurate historical account of the life of Jesus and the early church. Of course, his accounts include countless healings by the miraculous power of God. Moreover, like the majority of believers at that time, it is most likely that Luke himself healed the sick through prayers of faith in the name of Jesus by the power of God and as a demonstration of Kingdom of Heaven.

It is said that, "God created medicine." No, He didn't. God created everything created, but medicine is a concoction of man. In its simplest form, it constitutes placing our trust in something other than God. If we contend that we are trusting God to work through the medicine, then we are, at best, double-minded. I have seen many Christians with life-threatening diseases claim that their act of faith in Jesus is to believe in the latest treatment for their condition or that God created a medical treatment for their healing. This approach rarely goes well for people, and often leads to death if the illness is severe. I have even experienced believers turning me down for healing prayer because they had placed their confidence so entirely in the medicine, even though they claimed to believe Jesus was healing them. Those using medicine to maintain "quality of life" have lost sight of the basic tenet of the Christian faith that if we cling to our life, we will lose it but if we give up our life for Jesus, we will save it. (see Matthew 10:39, 16:25; John 12:25) Believing Jesus includes believing Him for everything He attained for us, including healing, at the expense of our own agenda for our lives.

For example, in addition to many other believers throughout history, John G. Lake, the healing evangelist, threw himself wholeheartedly into the hands of God whenever he became ill because he was so adamantly opposed to medicine as a false trust. In total submission to God, Lake resolutely believed in God's healing and also believed that if God had plans for his life, then God would need to make him well so that he could do God's will.[1] Similarly, when the Apostle Paul faced death repeatedly, he said he learned not to rely on himself but on God, who raises the dead. (see 2 Corinthians 1:9) This is what faith looks like in a Savior who already paid for our healing and is able to sustain us as we carry out His will.

In addition to this, Babylon (which is representative of the world system ruled by the evil one and his delegates), will deceive the nations with sorcery or witchcraft in the end times. (see Revelation 18:23) The word for *sorcery* or *witchcraft* in this passage in Biblical Greek is *pharmakeia. Pharmakeia* means *the use or administration of drugs or medication, i.e. "pharmacy,"* can also mean *magic potions or spells*, and is the same word Paul uses to describe witchcraft as an act of the flesh. (see Galatians 5:20) By definition, medicine is a mixture of ingredients blended together in specific proportions for the purpose of creating a desired effect on the body, which is very similar to the definition of a potion. Moreover, most medicines succeed in creating a certain desired result but cause damage to other parts of our bodies over time or create addictions and dependencies. This can be problematic because if we become dependent on anything other than Jesus for the maintenance of our health, then we have made ourselves vulnerable to deception by our need for something other than God to which we have become addicted. Eventually, as the end times come into fuller effect in this world, only those who take the mark of the beast will be able to participate in any form of commerce and this will undoubtedly include paying for medical care. (see Revelation 13:17) While I am not one who lives my life paranoid about the end times, I do know that we are closer to the return of Jesus than we have ever been. Therefore, all of this is to say that while there is still time, it would be beneficial for all of us to start building our faith and learning how to trust God and receive our healing directly from Him.

It is said that, "God created natural remedies." Not exactly. God created everything created and He created our bodies to be sustained, maintained, and healed by Him. What I mean by remedies is anything non-medicinal such as vitamins, supplements, or anything grown in

[1] See *Collected Works of John G. Lake*

nature, including foods, that we deliberately use for the purpose of maintaining our health or being made well. Just because a natural remedy may not be chemically produced does not mean that we are not placing our trust in something other than Jesus or worshiping creation rather than the Creator. (see Romans 1:25)

For example, for a while, the people of Israel enjoyed the healing effects of the marvelous "Balm of Gilead." This was a natural balm that exuded from the trees in the region of Gilead and was renowned for its healing properties. However, when the sin of the people grew beyond repair, the Balm of Gilead and all the physicians among God's people were powerless to heal anyone. (see Jeremiah 8:22) Only repentance and turning to God could heal their wound. On this note, I have heard many people pray, "the balm of Gilead" in their prayers for the sick, and this makes absolutely no Biblical sense. Firstly, the Balm of Gilead was an actual natural substance, not a spiritual metaphor, and most importantly, it is the blood of Jesus that heals us and sets us free.

It is said that, "Diet and exercise are the way to health and long life." No, our health does not come from diet and exercise—it comes from God. Jesus told His disciples not to worry about what we will eat or what we will wear because these are the things that dominate the thoughts of unbelievers. (see Matthew 6:32) The Apostle Paul said that the god of unbelievers (even if they profess to be believers) is their stomach. (see Philippians 3:19) This means that if your thoughts are dominated by food and what you are going to eat, then you are living like an unbeliever. However, if we seek first the Kingdom of God and His righteousness, then we begin living like a child of God and everything we need will be added to us. (see Matthew 6:33) Training our bodies and eating well are of some value, but godliness is of greater worth and we can live on the Word of God and doing His will. (see 1 Timothy 4:5-8; Deuteronomy 8:3; John 4:34) In other words, if Jesus is our Yeshua who heals and sustains us, then eating certain foods and abstaining from others in order to achieve desired results for our bodies can be an erroneous form of religion and is actually vanity, self-absorption, and unbelief.

To illustrate this, consider people you know who have eaten a healthy diet and have exercised their whole lives only to die of a heart attack at age fifty, and others you know who have eaten a very poor diet, drink an excess of alcohol, and smoke cigarettes yet live to a ripe old age. The first known monk, Antony, lived a life of devotion to God in a barren wilderness, eating and drinking only bread, water, and occasional salt. He lived to be one hundred and five years old.[2] Also, let's not forget that God sustained the whole nation of Israel in health for forty years on a diet of bread from heaven and miracle water. Elisha purified poisoned stew and undrinkable water with the command of God, and our prayers can sanctify our food in the same way. (see 2 Kings 2:22, 4:41; 1 Timothy 4:5) God blesses the food of the righteous, is able to bless whatever food we eat for the nourishment of our bodies, and one of the signs that follows believers is that we can even eat poison and not be harmed. (see Exodus 23:25; Mark 16:18) I'm not saying you should go out and try it but simply that we must have faith to believe it. If nothing else, it will cause us to be much less fussy and demanding about what we eat.

While eating is a necessity of life here on earth, we can keep food in its rightful place. Turning to food or eating for comfort can stunt the work of the Holy Spirit in our lives and overeating is typically a lack of self-discipline. In fact, many eating and exercise disorders are spiritually rooted in self-loathing, shame, condemnation, and control and are often the result of demonic oppression. God appointed a Comforter for us, the Holy Spirit, who empowers us with self-control in all things as a natural bi-product of allowing Him to guide us. (see John 14:26; 2 Timothy 1:7; Galatians 5:23) Unclean spirits can be expelled by the power and authority that believers have in the name of Jesus, and food issues will be driven away as we allow the Holy Spirit to help us receive God's love and compassion for us more deeply. Then, even our eating is done for the glory of God as He sustains us for His purposes.

It is said, "We have to be good stewards of our bodies." Yes, it is true that we are stewards of our bodies, which are the Temple of God and the host of the Holy Spirit who dwells within us. (see 1 Corinthians 6:19) However, in the context of this passage, Paul is discussing not abusing our bodies through sexual immorality or to fulfill personal lusts while

---

[2] From *The Sayings of the Desert Fathers* and public sources

recommending abstinence from sex outside of marriage between one man and one woman. This stewardship rationale is most often put forth by believers seeking to justify their pursuit of methods other than faith for healing but Paul goes on to say that we are not our own because we have been bought by God with the precious blood of Jesus, and exhorts us to glorify God with our bodies. The singular best way to glorify God with our bodies is to trust Him enough to offer our bodies to Him as an act of worship and by doing things with our bodies that are pleasing to Him. Faith pleases Him. (see Romans 12:2; Hebrews 11:6) Taking it to the highest levels of purity, Paul's approach to stewarding his body was to keep it in constant subjugation to Christ so that nothing would distract Him from fulfilling God's purpose for his life. (see 1 Corinthians 9:27)

We were not made to serve the demands of our bodies—our bodies were made to serve us and to serve God's purposes. If we claim that being a good steward of our body includes pumping it full of medicines, which are often toxic or poisonous, so that we can maintain some semblance of life or health, or that we are trusting God by developing dependencies on remedies and special diets, then we are self-deceived. This is not how God heals or sustains us and this is not God's idea of faith or good stewardship.

All of this said, I am certainly not encouraging any of us to die of foolishness by denying treatment when our faith is not strong enough to receive the healing we need from God. The Holy Spirit can lead us to certain temporary solutions that bring us relief. Until our faith is strong enough to receive our healing directly and supernaturally from God, medicine and remedies may be used. For example, God spoke to Isaiah about making a poultice of figs to cure King Hezekiah's skin boil, and Paul encouraged Timothy to drink a little wine to aid his chronic stomach issues. (see Isaiah 38:21; 1 Timothy 5:23) When we use this kind of approach by obeying the Holy Spirit, God will often accelerate our healing and bless our recovery. This said, we must stay attentive to the Holy Spirit's leading step by step and day by day. The Lord may lead us to do certain things that are beneficial for our health or recovery but He will never lead us into a dependency, addiction, or religious bondage. If we begin to place our faith in His solution rather than in Him, we will find the solution quickly losing its beneficial effect. Also, we must refrain from recommending or imposing what the Holy Spirit says to us as the solution for someone else. God as our Physician knows each of us and our bodies uniquely and individually, and He treats us accordingly with totally customized care.

God loves us as His children. Because of the blood of Jesus, there is no condemnation for us even when we require the use of medicine and remedies. However, let us be honest with ourselves and with God when we are trusting in other methods and admit that they are alternatives to wholeheartedly trusting God for divine supernatural healing. As our one and only Savior, Deliverer, Healer, and Sustainer, it is not God's will for us to be dependent on anything or anyone but Him. This includes medicine, remedies, special diets, vitamins, support groups, and anything else that would result in our demise if we discontinued partaking of them. Please consider this as you embark on your journey of faith for receiving healing from God. It is God's will for you to be well and Jesus already paid the bill.

Health Assessment

Take a moment, if you will, to take an honest assessment of your present health. Is your body in perfect condition? If not, what ails you?

Next, take another assessment of your present health, subtracting the benefits of any medicine, vitamins, remedies, and special diets that you may be using. Without the assistance of medicine and remedies, is your body in perfect condition? If not, what ails you?

Now, you have an honest baseline appraisal of the true, unassisted, condition of your health. I am not suggesting that you immediately cease using medicine and remedies, but I do want you to be aware of the things God is willing and able to heal you from so that you can begin to seek His healing and be healed.

Therefore, start today by listening to the Holy Spirit and doing what He says. Try doing something you have not been able to do as an act of faith. If you fail, try again in the future. Begin to trust God for your healing by offering your body to Him as an act of worship. You will be blessed.

In Real Life

At one point in my life, I was allergic to pork for fifteen years. When I would eat pork, my pupils would dilate, I would feel woozy, and from time to time I would pass out. Believe me, over the course of fifteen years, there were many jokes made about my love for the Jewish people and my pork allergy. Nevertheless, it was something I believed God wanted me healed of and so, from time to time, I would eat a little pork as an act of faith to see what happened. For several years, I tried this every once in a while with no evidence of healing. Then one week, a pastor and his wife invited me to their home for dinner. I was about to inform them in advance about my pork allergy, but the Holy Spirit stopped me. If by chance they served pork, I was going to eat it as an act of faith. At the same time, my hostess was listening to the Lord for what to serve for dinner, and He told her to serve a pork loin. When I arrived and saw the beautiful pork loin, my heart sank. Without trying to be obvious while I was carrying on normal conversation, I went into fervent prayer deep in my inner man. As the pastor prayed over our meal, it became fixated in my mind that he had to say the word, "sanctified" and by God's grace, he did. Nobody else knew what was happening, so I ate a big piece of pork loin as an act of faith as if pork had never been a restricted food for me. I was healed. I now enjoy pork whenever I want it in all of its various forms. Praise God!

A similar thing happened in my struggle with Candida. After the Lord revealed to me that I had Candida, I discovered that since there is no cure for Candida the only solution is to adopt a strict diet. However, if you recall, in my walk of total dependence on the Lord, I have had little to no control over my diet and have eaten with gratitude whatever He provides. Most of the things I was eating on a regular basis were the exact foods that were strictly forbidden for Candida sufferers. This meant that, in the beginning, there was a conscious exertion on my part to eat these foods as an act of faith. My faith was not in my food, but in God's healing. As I mentioned in another chapter, God healed me of Candida without following any special dietary restrictions. Now I eat anything and everything as an act of faith. God is good!

One fun story from when I first renounced medicine and remedies at the

Holy Spirit's prompting was when I cut my finger with a kitchen knife. When I had suffered cuts in the past, I would put antibiotic ointment on the cut and cover it with a bandage. But this time when I went to do this, the Holy Spirit stopped me and pointed out that even the ointment was a remedy. So instead, I decided that anything ointment can do, the blood of Jesus can do far better. So, I commanded bacteria to leave in the name of Jesus and bandaged my finger. My finger was completely healed when I took the bandage off. Hallelujah!

This creates a good interlude to bring up taking Communion for healing as we talked about in Chapter Six of this book. Medicine and remedies do not contain the life of God the way the body and blood of Jesus do. Try taking communion in the place of medicine and remedies and see what God does.

One time before the Lord asked me to renounce all medicine and remedies, I seemed to be worn down and sought the Lord for counsel. He told me that I had an iron deficiency and to acquire a certain type of iron supplement at a natural food store. (This is part of why I know the Lord can lead people in this way if they are not yet ready to receive supernatural healing.) I went to the store and purchased the vitamins. They were high quality and more expensive than most vitamins, but I was pleased to obey the Lord. I took them and my problem went away. About a month later, I met with a friend who told me all about her frustration with health struggles and how she had been through many medical tests. Eventually, she found a very expensive naturopathic doctor who diagnosed her with an iron deficiency. The course of treatment that was working for her was to take a combination of several of their special kind of vitamins that each cost ten times what I had paid for my supplements. Needless to say, this experience really highlighted some of the benefits of listening to the Holy Spirit! No tests, less expense, better results, no frustration. Praise God!

This said, another friend of mine who was aware that God had asked me to renounce all medicine and remedies decided that she wanted to try the same thing, particularly because finances were tight and she was dependent on expensive medication. She decided not to refill her prescription and trust God. In part, her motive was good, but it was a step of faith that God had not asked her to take, and so it was more a step of presumption. As she declined and weakened, it became evident that it was best for her to resume her medication for the time being. However, the experience propelled her to deeper faith. Each year since this, as she has continued to look to Jesus for healing, her medication has been incrementally decreased to almost half of what the dosage used to be. We both believe that someday she will no longer need any medication.

Another friend of mine had been on prescription anti-depressants for several decades and decided it was time to trust God to help her emotional issues. Instead of ceasing from her medication all at once, she decided to taper it off gradually, lowering the dose at certain intervals of time or as the Holy Spirit directed her. Every time she decreased the medicine, which had only served to suppress the wounds and oppressions that were in her, she would suffer from some kind of panic or anxiety attack. Instead of increasing her dose again, she trusted the Lord and occasionally called me for ministry and casting out demons that had plagued her for far too long. Today, she is completely off her medication, totally free of oppression, and living as a daughter of the Most High God. Hallelujah!

As for me, I try to eat a balanced diet and I exercise regularly because I enjoy being fit as it allows me to stay more alert spiritually. I experience no guilt or remorse if I eat something that has been condemned by the latest food trends or if I miss several days of exercise. If sickness comes into my life, medicines or remedies no longer tempt me, and I do nothing to alter my diet or exercise. I seek the Lord in prayer in the secret place and if I really need a breakthrough of faith for healing, I fast. On a side note, some illnesses can be cured by fasting. Not only does fasting expel our unbelief as we have discussed in prior chapters, it also gives our organs time to rest and reset, allowing them to repair and restore our bodies the way that God designed them to work. All of this is to say that I trust God as my Healer, and if healing does not seem to come readily I position myself to trust Him more. I truly believe that He loves us and He is willing, able, and will heal us if we let Him. We have no need of anything or anyone else.

Chapter Sixteen
BIRTHS & DEATHS

God is completely sovereign over life and death. (see Deuteronomy 32:39; 2 Samuel 2:6) There is a time to be born and a time to die, and our times are in His hands. (see Ecclesiastes 3:2; Psalm 31:15) God is the author of life who gives life to everything, and He knit each one of us together in our mother's womb. (see Acts 3:15; 1 Timothy 6:13; Psalm 139:13) God knew us, called us, and chose us before the foundation of the earth and every day of our lives is written in His book. (see Ephesians 1:4; Jeremiah 1:5; Psalm 139:16) The death of His saints is precious in His sight, and He takes no delight in the death of the wicked. (see Psalm 116:15; Ezekiel 18:23) Not even a sparrow falls to the ground without God knowing it. (see Matthew 10:29)

Births

When Eve gave birth to the firstborn of mankind, she rightfully said, "With the help of the Lord, I have brought forth a man." (see Genesis 4:1) Every birth since then has been equally brought about with the help of God in accordance with His will. Whether conception was planned or unexpected, it does not happen without God's authoring it. This means that if you have conceived a child, you have received a gift from God. (see Psalm 127:3) In fact, if God has ordained us to have natural born children, we will have them. Even if we have a medical condition that makes it improbable and the doctors say that it is impossible. Even if we are well along in years, beyond the points of childbearing. Even if we have taken measures to prevent conception...if God has ordained children for us, we will conceive.

Including Jesus, there are eight specific miracle births in the Bible. Abraham's wife, Sarah, was completely barren and well past the age of childbearing. Yet, at age ninety, she conceived and gave birth to Isaac. (see Genesis 11:30, 17:17, 21:2) Isaac's wife, Rebekah, was also barren until Isaac prayed for her so that she conceived and gave birth to Esau and Jacob. (see Genesis 25:21) Jacob's beloved wife, Rachel, was barren and she remained childless until the Lord remembered her and blessed her with a son, Joseph. (see Genesis 29:31, 30:32) Many years later, during the time of Judges, a man named Manoah had a wife who was barren until an angel of the Lord appeared to her giving her instructions about the lifestyle ordained for her unborn son. When she gave birth to him, she named him Samson. (see Judges 13) Elkanah, the Ephramite, had a wife named Hannah who was childless. Hannah was tormented by Elkanah's other wife about her barrenness, so she went to the Tabernacle of God to pour her heart out to the Lord and promised to dedicate her son to Him. The High Priest blessed Hannah, and she soon gave birth to Samuel. (see 1 Samuel 1:2, 9-20) Much later in history, the priest Zechariah and his wife, Elizabeth, were childless and "well along in years." An angel of the Lord appeared to Zechariah and told him that they would have a son, and soon Elizabeth gave birth to John the Baptist. (see Luke 1:11-25, 57-63) Finally, when God ordained for His own Son to be born, He selected a virgin named Mary who was a young woman of great faith. The angel Gabriel visited her and told her that the Holy Spirit would come upon her and she would conceive a son, even though she had never been with a man. In due time after this, she gave birth to Jesus the Son of God. (see Luke 1:26-38, 2:7)

Through our faith in Jesus, we have been redeemed from the curse of the Law, which includes barrenness, stillbirths, and miscarriages. Sometimes what we refer to as infertility, which is the same as barrenness, is more a matter of God's appointed timing in our lives and our families than a sign that it is not His will for us to have natural-born children. If we believe it is God's will for us to have natural-born children, and yet we remain childless, we can continue to press on in faith and not give up. Part of living for Him is offering our bodies to Him as a living sacrifice for His will to be done, not managing our bodies so that we can carry out our own plans for our lives. As a word of caution, David's wife Michal was struck barren due to the fact that she despised the way David extravagantly worshipped God. (see 2 Samuel 6:23)

In view of this, it is unnecessary to use scientific methods to procure conception. It is also unadvisable to interfere with God's will for our lives through pills or procedures that prevent us from conceiving or carrying to the point of birth. Preventing or aborting a pregnancy on our own accord, no matter the reason, is presumptively taking life and death into our own hands. If we have already conceived and it seems that our unborn child is to be stillborn or miscarry, we can believe God and receive resurrection life into our unborn or stillborn child so that they can live. If we do miscarry, have a stillborn child, or have aborted a pregnancy, there is no condemnation for us and we are not under God's curse. However, there may be room for us to grow in our faith and understanding of God's good and perfect will for our lives.

If the Lord prompts us to adopt children, it is a marvelous thing. God loves adoption, and He adopted millions of children—namely, us who believe Jesus! (see Ephesians 1:5) However, if we are convinced it is God's will for us to have our own children, then even if we adopt we can continue to believe God for natural children for as long as we have faith for conceiving.

Lifespan

The God ordained lifespan of man is 120 years. (see Genesis 6:3) God decreed this lifespan in the days of Noah when, prior to this, the average life lasted approximately 900 years. Later, Moses said that 70 years or even 80 years was the expected lifespan of God's people. (see Psalm 90:10) However, Moses lived to 120 years old himself, but he observed the deaths of a whole generation cursed to die in the wilderness due to their unbelief. All of this is to say that if we are not yet 70 or 80 years old at minimum, then we must do anything and everything to position ourselves in faith in agreement with God's will for us to live long lives and have strength equal to our days. (see Deuteronomy 33:25)

This said, obviously, not everyone lives to be 120 years of age. Therefore, we should examine the ways that we shorten or lengthen our lives. The first incident of a reduction in lifespan took place in the Garden of Eden when Adam and Eve ate from the tree of the knowledge of good and evil and forfeited everlasting life with God. (see Genesis 3:17-19) Later, when God shortened the lifespan of man from 900 years to 120 years, an 87% reduction, He explicitly said that His Spirit was no longer willing to strive or contend with man. Unfortunately sometimes, when believers are faced with difficult circumstances in matters of their health, even though they claim to believe Jesus for healing, their actions evidence striving with God and an unwillingness to do whatever it takes to break through to real faith. When they die as a result of their illness or demonic oppression, I believe it is a mercy from God and an act of His compassion to put an end to their striving, even though their life was much shorter than it should have been. Even God's people perish for lack of revelation of what Jesus has done and a lack of knowing God as He truly is. (see Proverbs 29:18; Hosea 4:6)

On the other hand, keeping the commandments of God and listening to His wisdom can add years to our lives and even multiply our years. (see Proverbs 3:1-2, 16, 4:10, 9:11, 10:27; Deuteronomy 11:21) King Hezekiah petitioned God from his deathbed on account of the ways He had obeyed God, and God added fifteen years to his life. (see 2 Kings 20:6) Plus, remember that when we petition God in the name of Jesus, we present His perfect obedience and righteousness on our behalf. Moreover, He has made our burden light by giving us only one command to obey by loving others as He has loved us.

Additionally, honoring our father and mother comes with a promise of long and good life, which carries into the New Testament without legalism. (see Exodus 20:12; Ephesians 6:2) To honor our parents means to give weight to the position they have in our lives and to hold them in good regard in the sight of others. As a side note, this is also part of why psychologizing our faith can be dangerous. After the original sin, there was the original blame. Adam blamed the wife God had given him for his own disobedience. (see Genesis 3:12) When we dig into our issues and blame our parents for our struggles, we are essentially doing the same thing. We must give our issues to Jesus, through whom we have been born again to a Heavenly Father, and learn to give an honest account of past events without dishonoring our parents, even in our hearts. We will be rewarded with long life here on earth for this, in addition to eternal life through faith in Jesus.

The point of all of this is to say that God knows the best path for our lives. Therefore, the best thing we can do for ourselves and our lifespan is to stop arguing with God, stop being double-minded or compromising between God's ways and the ways of this world, and allow God to transform us in our mind, will, and emotions so that we can do His perfect and pleasing will and have strength equal to our days.

Deaths

Death was never God's intention for mankind. When death was first introduced, it was a punishment and a mercy from God. It was a punishment because Adam and Eve had eaten from the wrong tree even though God told them that death would be the consequence for doing so. It was a mercy because after Adam and Eve ate from the wrong tree, God prevented mankind from eating from the Tree of Life so that we will not live forever in this fallen world in these mortal bodies. Even in view of this, we do not always know exactly what God is doing or why someone passes away before their time. The point is not for us to understand everything, but to remain in faith that God is good, God is fair in justice, and He is always more merciful than we could ever imagine.

In addition to this, God has thoroughly conquered the one who had the power of death through the sacrifice of His Son, and He is able to rescue the righteous from every sort of perilous situation. (see Hebrews 2:14; Psalm 68:20; 2 Peter 2:9) Through our faith in Jesus, we once again have access to the source of everlasting life, even though we will not live forever in these mortal bodies. Accordingly, a proper New Covenant death for believers is falling asleep or martyrdom for our faith in Jesus—not sickness. It is not God's will for us to die of an illness that Jesus took upon Himself at the cross. Our job is to believe that it is God's will for us to live out all of our days, even up to 120 years, and to receive it as God's blessing in our own life. Even in death, the righteous seek refuge in God. (see Proverbs 14:32)

Sometimes people die on account of their own sin or the sin of someone else. Ananias and Sapphira were both instantly struck dead for lying to the Holy Spirit, and King Herod was suddenly and publicly eaten by worms when he received glory from men rather than giving glory to God. (see Acts 5:1-11, 12:23) Two of Judah's sons died on account of their wickedness, and two of Aaron's sons were consumed when they entered the Tabernacle with unauthorized incense. (see Genesis 38:7-9;

Leviticus 10:1-2) The ten spies of Israel who gave a bad report about the Promised Land were instantly struck with a plague and died, in addition to other death plagues among the Israelites in the wilderness due to disobedience. (see Numbers 14:37) Those who rebelled with Korah against Moses' leadership were swallowed up by the earth. (see Numbers 16:32) Nabal, the fool who treated David with great contempt, suffered from his heart dying within him so that he turned to stone and died ten days later. (see 1 Samuel 25:36-38) Uzzah died instantly when he reached out to touch the Ark of God because he was not a Levite. (see 2 Samuel 6:7) When David called for an unordained census of the people to assess the strength of his army rather than trusting in the strength of God, 70.000 people died on account of David's sin. (see 1 Chronicles 21:14)

Nevertheless, Jesus strictly warned against searching for the sins of others as the reason for their untimely death because the only thing that really matters is for us to repent and trust in Him. (see Luke 13:1-5) Through faith in Jesus, we have been redeemed from all causes of untimely death. In the event of an untimely death, God is most likely functioning in ways that are higher than we may be aware of and that are true to His loving and merciful nature. For example, after King David's adultery, Bathsheba gave birth to a son who became very sick. David fasted and prayed to the Lord with many tears, but the child died. (see 2 Samuel 12:15-19) This seems like a harsh punishment, but it was also merciful. This is because a child born of illegitimate birth would never have been allowed to enter the Tabernacle of God, David's favorite place on earth. (see Deuteronomy 23:2) This would have caused David years of heartache or may have caused David to stumble into sin by allowing his son to enter the tabernacle, which may have led to his son's death. The most merciful thing God could do was to take the child to eternal life (where David knew he would eventually go to him) and grant David and Bathsheba another son, born in the covenant of marriage, who would be David's successor and the one appointed to build God's Temple in Jerusalem. (see 2 Samuel 12:23, 24) Other times, God has ended the lives of the righteous to protect them from seeing the evil in this world or the calamity that is about to come in the earth. (see Isaiah 57:1-2)

When a Christian dies an untimely death, it is better not to make up non-Biblical excuses like, "God healed them in heaven." There is no healing in heaven because there is no sickness in heaven, and our bodies remain on earth until the final resurrection from the dead. (see 1 Corinthians 15:23; 1 Thessalonians 4:14-17) Instead, let us be honest, humble, and mature enough to admit that somewhere there was a failure of faith, either on their part or ours, to believe and receive what Jesus died to give them. Nevertheless, we can trust that if the person was a believer, they are absent from their body but are present with the Lord. (see 2 Corinthians 5:8)

Jesus conquered death for us and all of us as the righteous in Christ can be absolutely fearless in the face of our own death and the death of others. We must never forget that God is able to raise the dead, not just at the resurrection, but in the here and now like Jesus did for Lazarus, Jairus' daughter, and the widow's son. (see John 11:43; Matthew 9:18-26; Luke 7:11-17) Furthermore, if (and only if) you are confident in your ability to hear the Holy Spirit and receive clear revelation from the Lord, there is a Scripture that petitions the Lord to, "Show me my end." (see Psalm 39:4) We can ask the Lord to reveal to us how we die so that we can be completely fearless in every situation we face that is not His ordained end for us. I have done this and the Lord has shown me a prophetic image of my death. Though I will not share the image with anyone, it has emboldened me in serving Him wherever He sends me.

Lastly, if martyrdom is God's will for our lives, as it was for all of Jesus' first apostles, many in the early church, and many of the most fervent believers throughout history, then a great eternal reward awaits us. Martyrs have a special place in the throne room of heaven, and those who have been beheaded for testimony of Jesus and the Word of God will rule and reign with Christ for 1,000 years. (see Revelation 6:9, 20:4) Martyrdom is not a premature death in the sight of God. His own Son died at age 33 after He had fulfilled God's purpose on this earth.

Accordingly, my prayer for myself and for everyone is to live out the fullness of our days because we are fulfilling God's purpose for our lives through our faith in Jesus. To Him be the glory forever in our births, in our lives, and even in our deaths!

Chapter Seventeen

WHAT DO YOU WANT ME TO DO FOR YOU?

Jesus has a way of getting straight to the point. On a few occasions when people came to Him, He asked them plainly, "What do you want me to do for you?" When He asked blind Bartimaeus this question, Bartimaeus unashamedly answered, "I want to see!" Jesus granted his request and immediately, the blind man could see. (see Mark 10:51-52)

What do you want Jesus to do for you? When we are pursuing the Lord for healing, it is good for us to be specific about what we want Him to do for us and to ask for the biggest miracle that we have faith to receive. Do you want Jesus to restore your youth like the eagle's? He is willing and able to do this. Do you want Him to grow you new limbs, eyeballs, ear canals, or body organs? He is willing and able do this. Do you want him to heal you of all disease, sickness, infirmity, infection, and oppression? He is willing and able to do this. Sometimes we just need to ask Him or tell Him what we want Him to do for us.

There are times when we don't have what we need because we haven't asked God for anything, or we ask for the wrong reasons, namely to suit our own desires. (see James 4:2-3) God knows if we want to be healed so that we can continue carrying out our own agenda for our life or abuse His grace to continue a life of sin. This said, because God's mercy through Jesus is so unfathomable, He may heal us in spite of sin and selfishness but do not be mistaken: His kindness is intended to bring us to repentance, deeper trust in Him, and obedience. As we submit ourselves to the leading of the Holy Spirit and step into alignment with God's will for our lives, we can ask for anything and know that it is already ours. (see John 15:16; 1 John 5:15) We do not obey God to earn His blessings—we obey God because, in light of all that Jesus has done for us, He is worthy of our trust and submission.

There are also times when we do not receive results from God because we have not asked for enough. For example, one time I was praying in my prayer closet for a man who was in need of healing from a prolonged illness, particularly in the face of an upcoming ministry trip. He knew that the Lord uses me to heal the sick through the laying on of hands but was unsure what he believed about this practice and, therefore, had not sought me out or asked me to pray for him. The Holy Spirit prompted me to send him a text explaining that sometimes the Lord asks, "What do you want me to do for you?" I was hoping he would respond by asking me to come and lay hands on him for healing. However, what he asked for was for the Lord to sustain his health on an upcoming ministry trip so he could minister effectively. So, I prayed for that and the Lord granted his request. However, he did not receive healing. This said, if he changes what he asks the Lord for, I am confident that he will experience different results.

Sometimes, people dangle themselves before God, waiting for Him to do something for them because they say, "He knows what I need." However, our need does not prompt God to heal us. Our need for salvation, deliverance, healing and sustenance prompted God to send His Son two thousand years ago to die on a cross to amply supply for all of our needs—including healing. There is a difference between helplessly praying casual or careless prayers to God hoping that He might somehow in some mysterious way bring about our healing compared to prayers of faith which truly press in to receive all that Jesus died to give us. We have to believe that Jesus paid for our healing through His death and resurrection, ask God to heal us, strive to enter into the shabbat shalom that Jesus gives us as a free gift, and receive our healing by engaging our faith to live as a healed person or testing out our healing by doing something that we should not be able to do.

Another approach people use is to grovel, beg, or bargain with God. But, we do not have to grovel or beg for something that God gives us as a free gift and we do not have to bargain with God by promising to be a good person or to do things for Him if He heals us. God is not fooled. If we were truly humbling ourselves before Him, we would have no need of making a spectacle of it and if we truly intended to do all these good things, we would already be doing them. More importantly, if we were truly praying in faith, we would not present ourselves to God as needy paupers but as His beloved children.

In fact, what God desires to have with all of us is a relationship of love between a heavenly Father and a beloved child, not a distant, vague, genie-in-a-bottle working-in-mysterious-ways-from-far-far-away kind of relationship. Intimacy and open communication between God and us is the primary reason He gave His Son as a sacrifice—so that we can know Him personally as our own Father. This means that sometimes, when we ask God to do something for us, He will respond with another question of Jesus such as, "Who do you say that I am?" As we have said before, matters of our health expose what we truly believe in our hearts about who God is and what Jesus has done for us. Do we know God loves us? Was Jesus just a nice guy or did He really pay the price for us to be completely saved, delivered, healed, and sustained? Oftentimes, we think that our illness or whatever other difficult circumstance we may be facing is the pinpoint of our problem. But really, the problem is that we do not deeply know the love of our Heavenly Father for us.

When we do know God's love for us as His children, we know that we do not have to fear that He has put sickness on us as punishment because no loving Father would ever do that. We do not have to fear that He will not heal us when we place our trust in Him because we know that, out of love for us, He is faithful to His word. We don't have to believe lies like, "Sometimes God heals, and sometimes He doesn't" because we know He loves us so much that He allowed His Son to be scourged, whipped, and crucified so that we could be made whole. God's healing is as certain as His salvation for everyone who comes to Him through faith in Jesus. It is His love that saved us. It is His love that expels all of our fears. It is His love that heals us.

What do you want Jesus to do for you? All things are possible for Him, and He has all authority in heaven and on earth and under the earth, both in this age and the age to come. (see Philippians 2:9-10; Ephesians 1:20-21) Like Bartimaeus, we can unashamedly ask the King of all creation for the healing we want without doubting that He is willing and able to do it for us. Jesus came to give us life and life to the full, and He taught us to pray for His will to be done on earth as it is in heaven where sickness is forbidden. (see John 10:10; Matthew 6:10) Our job is to believe this, put it into practice, and not settle for less than seeing it manifest in our lives.

What do you want Jesus to do for you? Everything is possible for the one who believes. When Jesus asked James and John this question, they asked to sit as his right and left hand. (see Mark 10:37) What boldness! Jesus did not reprimand them for their request but simply told them it was not His to grant. Similarly, if we ask Jesus for something that He is unable to do for any reason, He will tell us. However, since Jesus has been granted all authority over all creation, in order for Him to be unable to answer or grant our request, we would have to ask for some pretty weighty eternal matters like assigning thrones in heaven and knowing the date of His return to this earth. (see Mark 13:32) This said, with no exceptions, healing is absolutely NOT on the list of things Jesus is unable or unauthorized to do for us. Jesus healed us two thousand years ago on the cross. By His wounds we ***were*** healed. It has already been authorized by God and finished by Jesus.

The truth is that without Jesus, we deserve bodies that do not function correctly, are chronically ill with every kind of infirmity and disease, and succumb to an early death. But, because of what Jesus has done, we receive health, wholeness, healing for all of our sicknesses, and eternal life. We just have to admit we don't deserve it, admit we need it, believe it is ours, and then receive it with humble faith in the grace and mercy of God who loves us and gives it to us as a free gift. On that note, I have heard it said that receiving the true Gospel could be compared to receiving a finely wrapped gift box tied with a beautiful large ribbon only to open the box and discover that inside is a bottle of mouthwash. How humiliating! In order for us to receive the gift with gratitude, we have to admit that we need it and that it is the solution to our problem.

What do you want Jesus to do for you? Tell Him. Ask Him. Don't be shy or ashamed. Boldly enter into the throne of grace through the blood of Jesus to receive mercy in your time of need. (see Hebrews 4:6) God loves you so much, and He desires for you to be well more than you could ever know. Believe it. Receive it. Be healed in Jesus' name to the glory of God! Amen!

Appendix

HEALING & QUICKENING SCRIPTURES

Proverbs 4:20-22 - My son, pay attention to what I say; turn your ear to my words. Do not let them out of your sight, keep them within your heart; for **they are life to those who find them and health to one's whole body**.

Exodus 15:26 - He said, "If you listen carefully to the LORD your God and do what is right in His eyes, if you pay attention to His commands and keep all His decrees, I will not bring on you any of the diseases I brought on the Egyptians, for **I am the LORD, who heals you**."

Exodus 23:25 - Worship the LORD your God, and His blessing will be on your food and water. I will **take away sickness** from among you...

Isaiah 53:4-5 - Surely He took up our pain and bore our suffering, yet we considered Him punished by God, stricken by Him, and afflicted. But He was pierced for our transgressions, He was crushed for our iniquities; the punishment that brought us peace was on Him, and **by His wounds we are healed**.

1 Peter 2:24 - "He Himself bore our sins" in His body on the cross, so that we might die to sins and live for righteousness; "**by His wounds you have been healed**."

Galatians 3:13 - **Christ redeemed us from the curse of the law** by becoming a curse for us, for it is written: "Cursed is everyone who is hung on a pole."

Psalm 91:3-7 NLT - For He will rescue you from every trap and **protect you from deadly disease**. He will cover you with His feathers. He will shelter you with His wings. His faithful promises are your armor and protection. Do not be afraid of the terrors of the night, nor the arrow that flies in the day. **Do not dread the disease that stalks in darkness**, nor the disaster that strikes at midday. Though a thousand fall at your side, though ten thousand are dying around you, **these evils will not touch you**.

Psalm 103:2-5 - Praise the LORD, my soul, and forget not all His benefits-- who forgives all your sins and **heals all your diseases**, who redeems your life from the pit and crowns you with love and compassion, who satisfies your desires with good things so that your **youth is renewed like the eagle's**.

3 John 1:2 - Dear friend, I pray that you may **enjoy good health** and that all may go well with you, even as your soul is getting along well.

James 5:15-16 - And the **prayer offered in faith will make the sick person well**; the Lord will raise them up. If they have sinned, they will be forgiven. Therefore confess your sins to each other and pray for each other so that **you may be healed**. The prayer of a righteous person is powerful and effective.

Mark 11:24-25 - Therefore I tell you, **whatever you ask for in prayer, believe that you have received it, and it will be yours**. And when you stand praying, if you hold anything against anyone, forgive them, so that your Father in heaven may forgive you your sins."

Psalm 107:19-20 - Then they cried to the LORD in their trouble, and He saved them from their distress. He sent out His word and **healed them**; He rescued them from the grave.

Psalm 30:2 - LORD my God, I called to you for help, and **You healed me**.

Matthew 10:1 - Jesus called His twelve disciples to Him and gave them **authority to drive out impure spirits and to heal every disease and sickness**.

Luke 10:19 - I have given you authority to trample on snakes and scorpions and to **overcome all the power of the enemy; nothing will harm you**.

Mark 16:17-18 - And these signs will accompany those who believe: **In My name they will drive out demons**; they will speak in new tongues; they will pick up snakes with their hands; and **when they drink deadly poison, it will not hurt them at all; they will place their hands on sick people, and they will get well."**

Psalm 6:2 - Have mercy on me, LORD, for I am faint; **heal me**, LORD, for my bones are in agony.

Psalm 41:3-4 - The LORD **sustains them on their sickbed and restores**

them from their bed of illness. I said, "Have mercy on me, LORD; **heal me**, for I have sinned against You."

Psalm 147:3 - **He heals** the brokenhearted and binds up their wounds.

Jeremiah 17:14 - **Heal me**, LORD, and I will be healed; save me and I will be saved, for You are the one I praise.

Life Giving/Quickening (ESV Translation[3])

Psalm 119:17 - Deal bountifully with your servant, **that I may live** and keep Your word.

Psalm 119:25 - My soul clings to the dust; **give me life** according to Your word!

Psalm 119:37 - Turn my eyes from looking at worthless things; and **give me life** in Your ways.

Psalm 119:40 - Behold, I long for Your precepts; in Your righteousness **give me life!**

Psalm 119:50 - This is my comfort in my affliction, that **Your promise gives me life**.

Psalm 119:77 - Let your mercy come to me, **that I may live**; for Your law is my delight.

Psalm 119:88 - In your steadfast love **give me life**, that I may keep the testimonies of Your mouth.

Psalm 119:93 - I will never forget your precepts, for by them **You have given me life.**

Psalm 119:107 - I am severely afflicted; **give me life**, O LORD, according to Your word!

Psalm 119:116 - Uphold me according to Your promise, **that I may live**, and let me not be put to shame in my hope!

Psalm 119:144 - Your testimonies are righteous forever; give me understanding **that I may live**.

Psalm 119:149 - Hear my voice according to Your steadfast love; O

[3] King James Version translates bolded text as "quicken."

LORD, according to Your justice **give me life**.

Psalm 119:154 - Plead my cause and redeem me; **give me life** according to Your promise!

Psalm 119:156 - Great is Your mercy, O LORD; **give me life** according to Your rules.

Psalm 119:159 - Consider how I love your precepts! **Give me life** according to Your steadfast love.

Psalm 119:175 - **Let my soul live** and praise you, and let Your rules help me.

John 6:63 - It is **the Spirit who gives life**; the flesh is no help at all. The words that I have spoken to you are spirit and life.

Romans 8:11 - If the Spirit of Him who raised Jesus from the dead dwells in you, He who raised Christ Jesus from the dead will also **give life to your mortal bodies through His Spirit who dwells in you**.

1 Corinthians 15:45 - Thus it is written, "The first man Adam became a living being"; the last Adam became a **life-giving spirit**.

2 Corinthians 3:6 - ...Who has made us sufficient to be ministers of a new covenant, not of the letter but of the Spirit. For the letter kills, but **the Spirit gives life**.

Galatians 3:21 - Is the law then contrary to the promises of God? Certainly not! For if a law had been given that could give life, then righteousness would indeed be by the law.

1 Peter 3:18 - For Christ also suffered once for sins, the righteous for the unrighteous, that He might bring us to God, being put to death in the flesh but **made alive in the Spirit**...

Ephesians 2:5 - ...Even when we were dead in our trespasses, **made us alive** together with Christ--by grace you have been saved...

Colossians 2:13 - And you, who were dead in your trespasses and the uncircumcision of your flesh, God **made you alive** together with Him, having forgiven us all our trespasses...

About the Author

Wendy Bowen was the ultimate Type A, workaholic, overachiever, and control-freak until she had a dramatic encounter with the Lord Jesus Christ. Since then, the Lord called Wendy to give away all of her possessions and live by faith, prayer, and obedience to His voice. She lives for the purpose of proclaiming the Gospel and building up the Church by teaching the Word of God, helping believers experience Jesus through the Holy Spirit, and equipping disciples in their Kingdom purpose. The Lord blesses her ministry with His manifest presence and with miracles, signs, and wonders.

www.activatedchurch.com

www.manifestinternational.com

Made in the USA
Monee, IL
01 September 2019